THEN AND NOW

NEW YORK CITY'S

CENTRAL PARK

BUILDING AMERICA: THEN AND NOW

The Alaska Highway

The Brooklyn Bridge

The Eisenhower Interstate System

The Empire State Building

The Hoover Dam

The New York City Subway System

New York City's Central Park

The Telephone: Wiring America

BUILDING AMERICA
THEN AND NOW

NEW YORK CITY'S CENTRAL PARK

LOUISE CHIPLEY SLAVICEK

New York City's Central Park

Chelsea House
An imprint of Infobase Publishing
132 West 31st Street
New York, NY 10001

Library of Congress Cataloging-in-Publication Data
Slavicek, Louise Chipley, 1956–
New York City's Central Park / by Louise Chipley Slavicek.
p. cm. — (Building America, then and now)
Includes bibliographical references and index.
ISBN 978-1-60413-044-7 (hardcover)
1. Central Park (New York, N.Y.)—History. 2. New York (N.Y.)—History. I. Title. II. Series.
F128.65.C3S55 2009
974.7'1—dc22 2008025548

Chelsea House books are available at special discounts when purchased in bulk quantities for businesses, associations, institutions, or sales promotions. Please call our Special Sales Department in New York at (212) 967-8800 or (800) 322-8755.

You can find Chelsea House on the World Wide Web at http://www.chelseahouse.com

Text design by Annie O'Donnell
Cover design by Ben Peterson

Printed in the United States of America
Bang NMSG 10 9 8 7 6 5 4 3 2 1

This book is printed on acid-free paper.

CONTENTS

A "Natural" Retreat in the Heart of Manhattan

With more than 25 million visitors each year, New York City's Central Park is the most visited urban park in the United States and one of the most visited in the world. The 843-acre green oasis in the middle of Manhattan Island also has the distinction of being the nation's first major metropolitan park built specifically for the enjoyment of the entire community, from humble factory hands to powerful business tycoons, overworked servant girls to pampered socialites. The enormous publicity surrounding Central Park's creation in the mid-nineteenth century inspired other cities across the country to build big landscaped parks of their own, including Forest Park in St. Louis and Lincoln Park in Chicago. Yet even today, more than a century after it first opened to the public, Central Park—with its breathtaking scenery and unique architectural structures—remains the most famous of all America's urban parks.

Designed in 1857 by the man who would eventually become America's best-known landscape architect, Frederick Law Olmsted, and his partner, the English-born architect Calvert Vaux,

New York City's Central Park *(above)* covers about 6 percent of Manhattan and is visited by more than 25 million people each year. Filled with meadows, ponds, and woods, the park was designed to furnish New Yorkers with a serene, natural retreat from the noise and frantic pace of city life.

Central Park was meant to provide harried New Yorkers with a tranquil "rural" escape from the hustle and bustle of city life. In keeping with that goal, Olmsted and Vaux's design plan for Central Park disregarded the formal gardens and stately fountains and statues that filled London's Hyde Park, Paris's Jardin des Tuileries, and other leading urban public spaces of the era. Instead, the two men's innovative scheme called for an interconnected series of artfully composed bucolic (rural) landscapes that consisted of sweeping meadows, lush woodlands, pristine lakes, and secluded ponds.

Turning Olmsted and Vaux's vision for Central Park into reality, however, would prove to be an extremely time-consuming, labor-intensive, and expensive undertaking. The city of New York had only been able to afford the huge mid-Manhattan plot in the first place because the tract's rocky, swampy, and uneven terrain had kept its price per acre relatively low. To create the scenic rural retreat that Olmsted and Vaux described in their design proposal, workers would need to remodel virtually every inch of the soggy, boulder-strewn site.

Olmsted and Vaux's rustic sanctuary in the heart of Manhattan—one of the biggest public works projects in New York history—was under construction for nearly two decades and ultimately cost the city $15 million (the equivalent of more than $250 million today). It also required the effort of thousands of skilled and unskilled laborers to complete. Toiling from sunrise to sunset every day of the week except Sunday, a small army of Irish and German immigrant workers drained mosquito-infested marshes and bogs; scooped out lakes, ponds, and streams; blasted away mammoth boulders and ridges with more gunpowder than was fired at the Battle of Gettysburg; spread thousands of cartloads of topsoil imported from Long Island and New Jersey; and planted more than a quarter billion trees, flowers, and shrubs.

The final result of all this backbreaking labor was a landscape so "natural" in appearance that unsuspecting visitors assumed the park's creators had had the good fortune to stumble on a site of astonishing natural beauty and variety. Thus, when the prominent nineteenth-century editor and reformer Horace Greeley toured Central Park, he was heard to exclaim approvingly of its designers, "Well they have let it alone better than I thought they would." Indeed, it seems likely that few of Central Park's countless visitors would have guessed that the long rectangular tract's shady glens, gently rolling meadows, and crystalline waterfalls were completely man-made.

Today, Central Park's tens of thousands of trees, eight bodies of water, and hundreds of acres of grasslands and woodlands provide both a cherished refuge for nature-starved urbanites and a vital habitat for many different kinds of wildlife, including nearly 300 species of birds. Although the two-and-a-half-mile-long strip of green in the heart of Manhattan's concrete jungle is almost entirely the product of human ingenuity and sweat, nature nonetheless flourishes in America's most celebrated urban park.

CHAPTER 1

"Give Us a Park"

By the middle of the nineteenth century, New York had become the largest city in the United States. Drawn by its flourishing port and business enterprises, each year tens of thousands of immigrants flocked to Manhattan from Europe. In 1800, just under 70,000 people lived in New York City; by 1850, that number had swelled to more than a half million.

The creation of Central Park was closely linked to this explosive growth. By mid-century, many of Manhattan's business and cultural leaders had concluded that their metropolis needed a grand, landscaped park on a par with those in London and Paris, a park worthy of New York's new status as one of the world's most populous and prosperous cities. At the same time, they were alarmed by the swiftness with which Manhattan's once plentiful forests and meadows were disappearing. Fearful that the entire island would soon be paved over, they were determined to secure a green space for all New Yorkers to enjoy before it was too late.

"NO PLACE TO WALK, OR RIDE . . . OR STROLL"

When the crusade for a large park in New York began in the mid-1800s, the city contained barely 100 acres of public green space. These included 17 small squares, a modest park near City Hall, and the Battery—a historic but poorly maintained park on Manhattan's southern tip. "There is no place within the city limits in which it is pleasant to walk, or ride, or drive, or stroll; no place for skating, no water in which it is safe to row; no field for baseball or cricket, no pleasant garden where one can sit with and chat with a friend, or listen to the music of a good band," complained one disgruntled resident.

In their quest for a "pleasant" place in which to walk or ride, many New Yorkers were reduced to visiting nearby rural cemeteries. With its many ponds, rolling hills, and winding paths, Green-Wood Cemetery in Brooklyn was a favorite destination for thousands of nature-starved Manhattan families. After the nearly 500-acre burial ground opened in 1838, so many New Yorkers began spending their Sunday afternoons at Green-Wood that the cemetery superintendents decided it would be a good idea to issue admission tickets.

New York City was not alone in its lack of a large public park: In 1850, not a single city in the United States offered its residents that amenity. America's dearth of urban green spaces stood in sharp contrast to Europe, where a strong public park movement had developed in the early 1800s. European capitals such as London, Paris, and Copenhagen were famous for their magnificent public gardens and parks. The vast majority of these had started out as the private hunting preserves and gardens of the aristocracy and had only gradually been opened to the general populace. Birkenhead Park near heavily industrialized Liverpool, England, was one of the few exceptions to this rule. Birkenhead, the first publicly funded urban park in the world, was specially created by the British government in 1847 to meet the recreational needs of local workers, particularly the growing number of laborers who

Manhattan's population exploded during the first half of the nineteenth century as immigrants flooded into New York City from Europe. As Manhattan became ever more crowded, some New Yorkers began to fear that the entire island would soon be paved over. To prevent that from happening, they began to campaign for the creation of a large public park in the heart of Manhattan.

ENGLAND'S BIRKENHEAD PARK

The first publicly funded park in history was designed in 1843 by Sir Joseph Paxton, a prominent landscape gardener and engineer from Liverpool, England. Birkenhead Park, situated on the Wirral Peninsula in northwest England, between the River Mersey and the River Dee, was constructed in one of Great Britain's most heavily industrialized and populous regions to provide a healthful and serene retreat for factory workers and their families. Paxton's chief aim in designing the park was to create a tranquil, rural landscape complete with gently rolling meadowland, lushly wooded ravines, and meandering streams.

Because the land on which Birkenhead Park was constructed was marshy and therefore poorly suited to agriculture, the British government was able to purchase the 125-acre tract relatively cheaply. Over a period of more than two years, a large workforce labored on the flat, muddy site, fashioning hills and valleys, draining marshes, digging artificial lakes, planting trees and shrubs, seeding meadows, laying out carriage drives and pedestrian paths, and building a lodge, boathouses, and bridges. When Birkenhead Park was officially opened by Chief Commissioner of Woods and Forests Sir George Howard on April 5, 1847, a crowd of 10,000—rich and poor, factory workers and factory owners alike—turned out to celebrate what would popularly come to be known as the "People's Park."

were forced to spend most of their waking hours in dark, airless factories.

TWO EARLY PARK CRUSADERS: WILLIAM CULLEN BRYANT AND ANDREW JACKSON DOWNING

In the summer of 1844, an ardent admirer of Europe's public parks, the poet and editor William Cullen Bryant, launched a campaign to convince his fellow New Yorkers that they needed a grand park of their own. New York was expanding so rapidly that Manhattan's once lush greenery would soon vanish altogether, Bryant warned in a special Independence Day editorial in his newspaper, the *New York Evening Post.* Land must be set aside for a park at once, he urged, while there was still undeveloped acreage left on the island. A few months later, Bryant praised the British government for providing its citizens with thousands of acres of public parkland, including more than 1,400 acres in London alone. "These parks have been called the lungs of London," he wrote in the *Post,* noting that overcrowded New Yorkers desperately needed some breathing space of their own.

In 1848, the movement for a large public park in New York City gained another well-known spokesman: the prominent landscape gardener Andrew Jackson Downing. For the next four years, until his death from drowning following a steamboat accident, Downing published one pro-park editorial after another in his journal, the *Horticulturalist.* (*Horticulture* is the art and science of cultivating flowers, vegetables, fruits, or ornamental plants.) In the editorials, he called for the construction of a 500-acre landscaped park in America's biggest city that would be modeled after London's mammoth Hyde Park. "What are called parks in New York are not even apologies for the thing; they are only squares or paddocks," Downing remarked disdainfully in one column. "Is New York really not rich enough, or is there really not land enough in America," he asked his readers in another editorial, "to give our citizens public parks of more than ten acres?"

Like Bryant, Downing was convinced that a spacious, treed park would enhance the physical well-being of New Yorkers by acting as the city's "lungs." If a park were properly designed and maintained, it could provide important cultural as well as health benefits to the people of Manhattan, he further asserted. Downing, who had a reputation for snobbery, worried about what he considered his countrymen's lack of cultural refinement. Art could play a vital role in making the rough young republic more civilized, he thought, and for Downing, well-landscaped parks were works of art on a par with the finest paintings or sculptures. Downing expected that a grand public park would be a source of cultural enlightenment and moral uplift for New York City's half million inhabitants, particularly its vast working class. "Every laborer is a possible gentleman," Downing once declared. By offering its visitors "the refining influence of intellectual and moral culture," he avowed, an artfully designed public space would "raise up the man of the working men to the same level of enjoyment with the man of leisure and accomplishment."

THE PARK MOVEMENT GAINS MOMENTUM

Year by year, the park campaign begun by Byrant and Downing grew. By 1850, two of New York's most celebrated literary figures, historian George Bancroft and essayist Washington Irving, had joined the crusade. Following the lead of the wealthy merchant and zealous park supporter Robert Bowne Minturn, by the start of the new decade many of Manhattan's most influential businessmen had also taken up the cause.

Minturn's interest in the park movement began in the late 1840s, when he and his wife, Anna Mary Minturn, toured Europe. The Minturns were appalled by what they considered the shameful contrast between the spacious, meticulously maintained European parks and New York's meager and all-too-often neglected public grounds. When Robert Minturn returned home, he immediately began to contact friends and business associates to discuss his concerns regarding New York's embarrassing lack of public green spaces.

Minturn had little difficulty convincing his wealthy acquaintances that New York required a park deserving of "the greatness of our metropolis." Yet a desire to make their city the equal of the European capitals was not the only reason that Minturn's well-heeled friends embraced the idea of a grand public park. Most historians agree that a wide range of motives inspired the upper-class New Yorkers who formed the backbone of the park movement after 1850.

A PLACE TO SEE AND BE SEEN

Most of the affluent merchants, bankers, and landowners who led the park campaign during the mid-1800s seem to have been as concerned about satisfying their own particular recreational wants as they were about enhancing the city's reputation in the world. Above all, they desired a fashionable and safe public place where they and their families could mingle and promenade with other members of New York's upper crust, away from the crowded, dusty streets of downtown Manhattan.

Securing an attractive and safe public area in which New York's social elite could see and be seen was especially important to Anna Minturn and the other well-off women who backed the project. "Respectable" females possessed few opportunities for public exercise and recreation in mid-nineteenth-century Manhattan. Earlier in the century, afternoon promenades on the city's wider thoroughfares, such as Fifth Avenue, Broadway, or the Battery, had been a favorite activity of many upper-class New York women. Yet, by the mid-1800s, these once stylish downtown locales had been transformed: "The very noticeable change has been produced," a *Post* reporter explained haughtily in 1851, "by the vast immigration of a foreign population." Modest female strollers now found themselves "stared out of countenance [self-composure] by whiskered and mustachioed chatterers," the correspondent noted with disgust. "But there is a remedy for all these inconveniences," he concluded. "Let the new park be secured at once." A spacious and well-regulated park, the reporter—and the project's female supporters—hoped, would provide New York's gentlewomen with a public spot where they could once again feel comfortable strolling and socializing.

Another form of recreation, aside from strolling, that the park's affluent supporters—male and female alike—hoped to enjoy in their grand new space was carriage driving. By the mid-

1800s, carriage ownership had become an important status symbol for wealthy city dwellers in Europe and the United States. Yet there were few places in New York where the city's carriage-

Affluent women took walks down some of New York's wider thoroughfares such as Fifth Avenue. These ladies, however, were soon deterred from their daily exercise as their preferred routes became busier and noisier with the influx of immigrants and new businesses. Frustrated with their lack of space, these wealthy women supported the campaign to build a public park.

owning elite cared to take their expensive and showy conveyances. By 1850, note Roy Rosenzweig and Elizabeth Blackmar in their history of Central Park, *The Park and the People*, "traffic, immigrant crowds, and dirty streets had impinged on the gentility of Lower Manhattan [carriage] promenades." A spacious landscaped park, the project's rich backers figured, would provide them and their families with a pleasant and safe place to roll about in their fashionable vehicles.

FOR THE HEALTH OF THE CITY

The park's wealthy supporters were not just convinced that a vast public park would improve the quality of their own and their families' lives; they also believed that a park would enhance the physical and moral health of New York's vast working class and the commercial health of the city as a whole.

By 1850, several decades of rapid industrial growth combined with a burgeoning population had turned much of the southern half of Manhattan into a congested and disease-ridden jumble of warehouses, factories, tenements, and boardinghouses. A spacious public park, the project's upper-class supporters argued, would offer Manhattan's hundreds of thousands of working class inhabitants a much-needed respite from the tainted air and cramped streets of their squalid urban neighborhoods. As Rosenzweig and Blackmar observe in *The Park and the People*, other measures—such as improved housing and sanitation—would have addressed the grave health issues that confronted New York City's masses more directly than did a public park. "Still," they write, "during muggy summer months in a fetid atmosphere of dust, coal smoke, and decaying manure and garbage, many naturally viewed fresh air and tree-filtered breezes as a primary source and certainly the symbol of physical well-being."

The park movement's genteel leaders were at least as concerned about the moral well-being of New York's working-class majority as they were about their physical well-being. A large public park, the project's promoters believed, would offer workers an appealing alternative to such popular—and, in their view, immoral—diversions as cockfighting, gambling, and drinking at the corner saloon. In contrast to the boisterous temptations of "brightly lighted streets," one park supporter confidently declared, a park would serve to encourage "*family* outings" and other "wholesome" forms of recreation among all classes of New Yorkers.

By helping to make New York a healthier and more wholesome place in which to live and raise a family, a spacious public park would also promote the city's commercial interests, the merchants, bankers, and landowners who spearheaded the park movement reasoned. New York's rapid industrialization and exploding immigrant population had spurred many middle-class and wealthy residents to abandon the city for nearby Brooklyn or

"A PERMANENT FOREST FOR THE ACCOMMODATION OF LOAFERS"

Not everyone in New York believed that the city needed a big new public park. Not surprisingly, many of Manhattan's leading real estate developers bitterly opposed the project. Government officials, they asserted, had no business withdrawing any property on Manhattan Island from private development. "There is no need of turning one-half of the island into a permanent forest for the accommodation of loafers," one critic of the project contended in the *Journal of Commerce*. "The grand park scheme is a humbug and the sooner it is abandoned the better."

Land reformers, labor unions and their supporters, and public health activists had their own objections to the park scheme. The outspoken land reformer Hal Guernsey thought that the city should purchase a big tract of land not for a public park but rather for a government-subsidized housing development to help New York's overcrowded masses. The New York Industrial Congress, a labor union that represented many of the city's factory workers, was also critical of the park proposal, blasting the idea of using taxpayer money to build a large park many miles north of

New Jersey. (Brooklyn was still a separate city in the mid-1800s; it would not become a borough—or administrative unit—of New York City until 1898.) A vast green oasis modeled after Europe's opulent public grounds, the park's boosters reasoned, would do much to offset the appeal of New York's less built-up rivals like Brooklyn and keep more affluent residents—and their money—in the city.

THE GOVERNMENT GETS INVOLVED

In 1851, the park movement gained a crucial ally when New York's new mayor, Ambrose Kingsland, formally backed the project. That April, Kingsland called on the Common Council to secure land for a park immediately, while suitable acreage could still

New York's major population centers as impractical and fundamentally unjust. It wanted the municipal government to instead construct numerous smaller parks in Manhattan's congested working-class neighborhoods, where public green spaces were most needed.

The German-language newspaper *Staatszeitung*, a firm advocate of the union movement and the working class, also preferred the use of tax money to fund "many smaller parks in different parts of the city" that "would be equally accessible and useful to all citizens" rather than the spending of public funds on one massive park that would benefit only "greedy speculators" and "codfish aristocrats" (newly rich social climbers). Leading New York public health activist Dr. John Griscom lent his backing to the "many small parks versus one large park" cause as well. Creating numerous little parks in the heart of downtown's lower-class districts in lieu of one huge public space in less-populated upper Manhattan, he declared, "would certainly be less aristocratic, more democratic, and far more conducive to public health."

An expensive carriage was an important status symbol in nineteenth century New York, but by the middle of the century well-off carriage owners had become disgruntled with the city's increasingly crowded and dirty streets. A large landscaped park, they hoped, would provide an attractive and safe spot for them to roll about in their showy vehicles.

be found on the island for a reasonable price. A spacious public park, he assured the members of the council, would be "a lasting monument to the wisdom, sagacity and forethought of the founders." The council, thus enticed, agreed to turn the matter over to its Committee on Land and Places for further consideration.

A few weeks later, the Committee on Land and Places came out strongly in favor of the mayor's pet project. The committee even went so far as to recommend a site for the new park, urging municipal leaders to seek state approval to purchase 150 acres of land on the Upper East Side, on what was then the northern edge of the city. Known as Jones Wood, the popular picnicking spot stretched north from 66th Street to 75th Street and west from the East River to Third Avenue. One admirer described the scenic riverside property as "a tract of beautiful woodland . . . thickly covered with old trees, intermingled with a variety of shrubs. The surface is varied in a very striking and picturesque manner, with craggy eminences and hollows and a little stream runs through the midst."

The committee's plan to locate the new park in Jones Wood soon hit a major roadblock, however. Although they no longer resided on the land, the property's owners, the Jones and Schermerhorn families, stubbornly refused to sell. The project's supporters, undeterred, pushed a bill through the state assembly that authorized New York City to take Jones Wood through eminent domain. (Eminent domain is the power of the state to seize private property for public use after compensation is provided to the owner.) On July 11, 1851, the Jones Wood Act was approved by the legislature in Albany. New York had officially committed itself to building a grand public park on Manhattan Island.

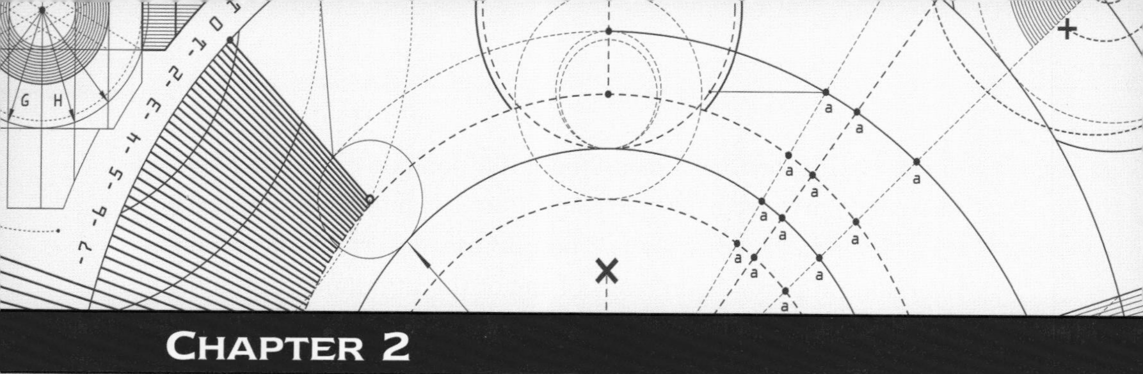

CHAPTER 2

Central Park It Is

Despite widespread support for the Jones Wood location in the Common Council and the state assembly, many leading New Yorkers did not view the scenic grove along the East River as the best site for their new park. Some, like Andrew Jackson Downing, thought it was too small. Downing wanted the city's new park to include at least 500 acres so it would be comparable in size to Europe's grand public spaces. Others, including a number of prominent West Side businessmen, landowners, and politicians, disapproved of Jones Wood's location on the eastern edge of Manhattan. A more centrally located park would better serve the majority of the island's residents, they maintained.

JONES WOOD VERSUS A "CENTRAL" PARK

In response to these concerns, in August 1851 the Common Council appointed a two-man committee to examine the suitability of the Jones Wood site. Six months later, the Special Committee on

Parks issued its findings: The size of the proposed Jones Wood park was inadequate for a city of more than a half million residents, and its eastern location was inconvenient. In lieu of Jones Wood, they recommended a mid-island site that stretched half a mile from Fifth to Eighth avenues and approximately two and one-half miles from 59th Street to 106th Street. At 778 acres, the long, narrow rectangle of land was nearly five times bigger than the Jones–Schermerhorn property. Despite the plot's mammoth size, the per-acre price was sure to be cheap, the committeemen assured the Common Council, because the tract's rocky and uneven terrain made it unsuitable for private development.

For the next two years, the mid-island plot's supporters competed with the Jones Wood faction to win political and popular backing for their site. The Jones Wood group contended that their location would be significantly cheaper to develop. In contrast to the rock-strewn and muddy mid-island acreage, Jones Wood would require little more than the clearing of a few paths to transform it into a functional and attractive park, they said. The mid-island site's supporters countered that it made no sense to build a park intended to serve all New Yorkers on Manhattan's easternmost fringes. By mid-1853, as the battle over the two sites dragged on with no apparent end in sight, many Manhattan residents had lost all patience with their government. That June, a columnist for the *Commercial Advertiser* spoke for thousands of his fellow New Yorkers when he admonished city and state officials to stop squabbling about the park and start building it: "Give us a park," he pleaded, "be it central, or sidelong, here, there, anywhere."

In July 1853, still unable to decide between the park sites, the state legislature passed two bills: one that authorized the city to take the mid-Manhattan plot through eminent domain, and a second that reauthorized it to acquire Jones Wood. Public outcry against the assembly's plan to fund two expensive parks in Manhattan was so great, however, that—in early 1854—legislators finally repealed the Jones Wood Act and committed New York to developing the central site alone.

A NEW STRUGGLE OVER CENTRAL PARK

The struggle over Central Park, as the mid-island plot was now officially known, was not over. Within months of their victory in the state assembly, Central Park's supporters found themselves embroiled in a new battle concerning the nearly 800-acre site. From 1854 to 1855, New York City was gripped by a major economic recession. With more than 15,000 workers unemployed and soup kitchens feeding some 12,000 people a day, many New Yorkers doubted whether the city could really afford such a large

SENECA VILLAGE

The most densely settled section of the Central Park site in the mid-1850s was Seneca Village, located between Seventh and Eighth avenues and 82nd and 89th streets on the western side of the park. The area was first settled in 1825 by a small group of free African Americans just two years before slavery was outlawed in New York State. Year after year the little village grew, until—by the middle of the nineteenth century—Seneca was a central pillar of New York City's African-American community. In 1855, the New York State Census recorded Seneca's population as 264, of whom more than two-thirds were black, and the village boasted a school and three flourishing churches. The village's most popular church, the African Methodist Episcopal Zion, was characterized by one contemporary New Yorker as the "largest and wealthiest church of coloured people in this city, perhaps in this country."

Although the majority of Seneca Village's residents resided in modest, one-story houses, their living conditions were often significantly better than those of the thousands of African Americans who resided in Lower Manhattan's squalid and cramped tenements. Villagers also park. In response, a campaign was launched in the Common Council to decrease the park's size.

Not everyone in the municipal government thought that reducing Central Park was a good idea, however. New York's new Democratic mayor, Fernando Wood, believed that shrinking the park would do more harm than good to the city's ailing economy by taking away hundreds of potential jobs from New York's hard-pressed working class. Consequently, when the Common Council voted in 1855 to whittle down the park's area by removing 12 blocks from its lower end and 400 feet from each side, Wood promptly vetoed the bill. A grand public park would not only furnish New Yorkers with an inspiring symbol of their growing city's

enjoyed a great deal more outdoor space than their counterparts in southern Manhattan, and many were able to supplement their diets and even earn a little extra income by cultivating small vegetable gardens or raising pigs or other livestock. In no other section of the park site did a greater proportion of residents own their own land; in the mid-1850s, more than 50 percent of Seneca's adult population owned the land on which they lived, making property ownership among Seneca's black residents five times greater than that among African-American New Yorkers as a whole, according to historians Roy Rosenzweig and Elizabeth Blackmar.

By the end of 1857, no more landowners—black or white—lived in Seneca Village, and every house, school, church, and shop in the once-thriving little town had been razed to make way for the city's grand new public park. Nearly a century and a half later, in 2001, park administrators placed a plaque at the site of Seneca Village to commemorate New York City's first significant community of African-American property owners.

"destiny now opening so brilliantly before us," Wood declared, it would also provide desperately needed employment to "many hundred workmen and laborers."

After two years of meticulously surveying and assessing the 17,000 lots that made up the mammoth Central Park site, in 1856 the city government finally authorized the payment of $5,069,694 to the tracts' 561 owners. One-third of that sum was to be covered by the landowners whose property adjoined the site, on the assumption that the value of their land would soar once the park was built. The remaining two-thirds of the purchase price was to be met by the city's taxpayers.

"SQUATTERS," "VAGABONDS," AND "SCOUNDRELS"

Before the rocky, swampy rectangle of land that the government had purchased for $5 million could be transformed into a landscaped park, the city would need to clear out the more than 1,600 men, women, and children who made their homes there. Most New Yorkers appeared to have little sympathy for the plight of the park dwellers, who were routinely dismissed in contemporary writings as "squatters," "vagabonds," and "scoundrels." The park's impoverished and chiefly Irish inhabitants resided in "rickety . . . little one story shanties . . . inhabited by four or five persons, not including the pig and the goats," the *New York Times* reported scornfully, while the *Evening Post* portrayed the park community as an unsavory hodgepodge of "gambling dens, the lowest type of drinking houses, and houses of every species of rascality."

For more than a century, the traditional depiction of Central Park's onetime residents as criminals, tramps, and loafers would go virtually unchallenged. All of that changed in the early 1990s, however, when historians Roy Rosenzweig and Elizabeth Blackmar published the results of their groundbreaking study on the 1,600 people who called the park home in 1857. By analyzing contemporary tax lists, church registers, land records, and

Although trained as an architect, Calvert Vaux *(above)* soon picked up the basic elements of landscape design from his employer and mentor, Andrew Jackson Downing. Together, they designed a large public area in Washington, D.C. Vaux later provided the winning design for Central Park with Frederick Olmstead.

censuses, Rosenzweig and Blackmar were able to construct the first detailed portrait of the park's much-maligned occupants. Fully 90 percent of the park dwellers were African Americans or recent immigrants from Europe—principally Irish or German—the historians determined. They also discovered that a majority of the park's adult residents were gainfully employed. More than two-thirds toiled at low-paying, unskilled jobs as day laborers, gardeners, or servants, and most of the remaining third were skilled tradesmen such as carpenters or stonemasons. Finally, the two scholars' findings suggested that far fewer of the park dwellers were squatters than had previously been assumed. According to Rosenzweig and Blackmar's research, one-fifth of the park's inhabitants owned their land, and a substantial portion of the rest probably had informal, verbal agreements with the property owners that gave them use of the land.

Eviction of the park dwellers—squatters, renters, and landowners alike—started soon after the site was surveyed and assessed in 1856 and was completed in late 1857. The final eviction orders could not have come at a worse time. In the autumn of 1857, New York was in the throws of a major economic crisis: Dozens of businesses and banks had closed their doors, and thousands of men and women were without work. Inevitably, the New Yorkers who were hardest hit by the economic downturn were also those with the least resources: the city's African-American and immigrant populations, the very same groups that made up 90 percent of the Central Park community. Yet whatever hardships the evicted park dwellers endured in the autumn of 1857 seem to have gone completely unnoticed by both the press and the general public.

According to author Eugene Kinkead in *Central Park: The Birth, Decline, and Renewal of a National Treasure*, not all of the park's residents went quietly. To convince the hangers-on to leave, Kinkead writes, "The Central Park Police was formed, consisting of a captain, three sergeants, and fifteen men. The battle was quickly joined. Falling back before the better discipline and armament of the lawmen, the squatters with their greater knowledge of the terrain waged stubborn guerrilla warfare with fusillades of bricks." By October 1, however, the last of Central Park's 1,600 residents had vacated their homes; work on New York City's great public improvement project could finally begin.

A COMPETITION IS ANNOUNCED

With the Central Park site cleared of all its human inhabitants, the park administrators' next task was to formulate a design for the craggy and irregular 778-acre plot. On October 13, 1857, a public competition for "laying out the park" was announced in the leading New York City newspapers. The contest, which had a closing date of April 1, 1858, offered prizes of $2,000, $1,000, $750, and $500, respectively, for the four best design plans. Its sponsor was the recently formed Board of Commissioners of the Central Park. Composed of 11 members, most of them prominent New York City businessmen or professionals, the board had been appointed by the state legislature in Albany a few months earlier to develop and manage the new park.

The idea for the contest—America's first-ever landscape design competition—had not come from the commissioners themselves. It was thought up by a talented and ambitious young architect named Calvert Vaux (pronounced "vox"). The diminutive Vaux, who stood just 4 feet 10 inches tall, had received his professional training in London. In 1850, at the age of 24, Vaux left his native England for Newburgh, New York, to work for the prominent park advocate and landscape gardener Andrew Jackson Downing. (The eighteenth- and nineteenth-century profession of landscape gardening focused on designing the grounds that surrounded public buildings and private estates. The term *landscape architecture*, which refers to the planning and design of natural and built environments, was not yet in general use in the United States.)

Vaux's main responsibility in Downing's Newburgh firm was to design houses and other architectural structures on the

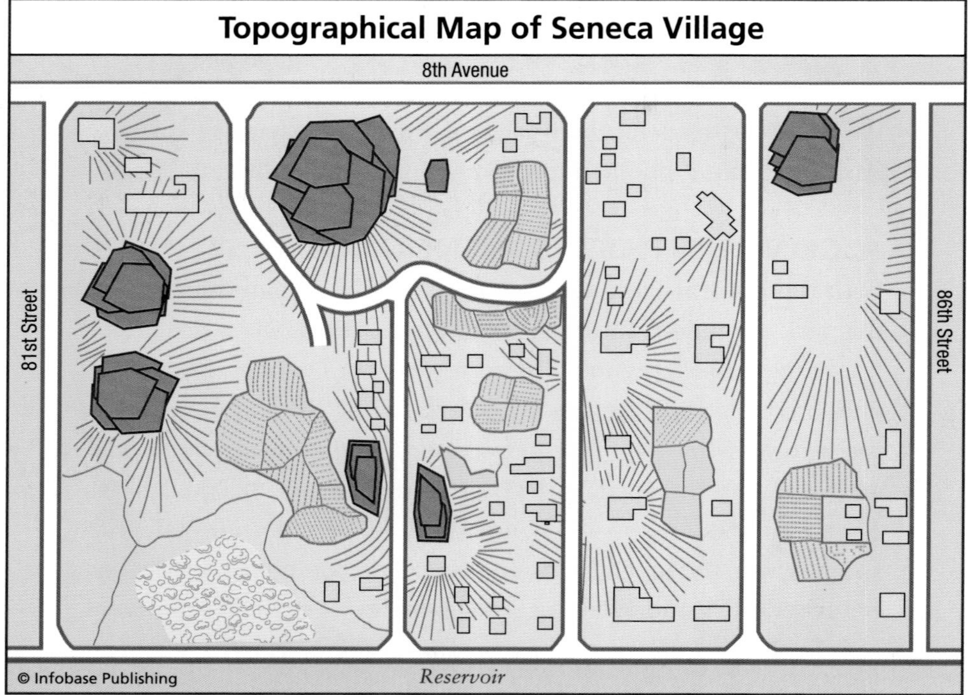

By the mid-1850s Seneca Village had become a central pillar of Manhattan's African-American community. While most black New Yorkers lived in crowded tenements in Lower Manhattan, the majority of Seneca Village's African-American residents owned their own homes. The village also boasted three churches and a school.

---

private estates of the horticulturist's wealthy clients. During his employment with Downing, however, Vaux was also able to learn the fundamentals of landscape design. Soon after Vaux arrived in the United States, he began to assist his new boss on major landscaping projects, including the design of formal public grounds for the Smithsonian Institution's first building—dubbed the "Castle"—in Washington, D.C. Following Downing's untimely death in a freak steamboat accident in 1852, Vaux ran his mentor's landscaping firm in Newburgh for several years before he moved to New York City in late 1856 to practice architecture.

Once in Manhattan, Vaux took an immediate interest in the public park project that had been so dear to Downing's heart. The Board of Commissioners, he soon discovered, was giving serious consideration to a design for the new park submitted by the project's engineer in chief, Egbert Viele, whose special expertise was in sanitary drainage systems (sewer systems). When Vaux, who had several acquaintances on the board, was given the opportunity to review Viele's plan, he was appalled. The engineer in chief's design completely lacked an "artistic conception,"

THE SISTERS OF CHARITY AND CENTRAL PARK

Aside from the fortress-like Arsenal that the State of New York erected at Fifth Avenue and 64th Street in 1848, the most impressive structures within the Central Park site belonged to the Sisters of Charity of St. Vincent de Paul, a Roman Catholic religious order. In 1847, the sisters purchased property on a small hill in what would eventually become the northeastern corner of the park. Soon the nuns had created a vibrant religious community on their little hill, which they dubbed Mount St. Vincent. By the time New York City acquired the Central Park site in the mid-1850s, the sisters' hilltop retreat included several buildings: a stately brick chapel, a boarding school for 200 young Catholic women, and a free day school for 50 children from nearby areas.

The Sisters of Charity were allowed to remain in the park two years longer than any of the tract's other residents. In 1859, however, the Central Park Commission finally evicted the nuns and turned their buildings into administrative offices. The nuns returned briefly to their former home during the Civil War, when they operated a military hospital in the old convent. Shortly after the war ended in 1865, the hospital was converted into a park restaurant and the brick chapel transformed into a statue gallery. Both buildings were destroyed in a fire less than two decades later.

Vaux declared, and—with no overarching aesthetic purpose to give form and meaning to a park visitor's experience—one section of the grounds would seem very much like another. (Aesthetics is the philosophical study of the various qualities perceived in works of art.) "Being thoroughly disgusted with the manifest [obvious] defects of Viele's plan," Vaux later recalled, "I pointed out whenever I had a chance that it would be a disgrace to the City and to the memory of Mr. Downing . . . to have this plan carried out." Before long, the earnest young architect had convinced the commissioners to set aside Viele's uninspired plan and resolve the design question via public competition instead.

Determined that Manhattan's new park should equal Europe's celebrated public grounds in the size, number, and variety of its amenities, the commissioners developed a number of specific requirements for the design entries. For example, each plan had to include a 20- to 40-acre parade ground for civic assemblies and militia drills, sites for a music or exhibition hall and an ornamental fountain, a 2- to 3-acre flower garden, a lookout tower, and a place where visitors could ice-skate in the winter. In addition, the board stipulated, all entries had to include a minimum of four east-west transverse (cross) roads so that non-park traffic could flow unimpeded across the narrow site.

CHOOSING A DESIGN

By the contest's closing date of April 1, 1858, 33 designs had been entered in the Central Park competition. All but two of the entrants were American, and just one—Susan Delafield Parish, a wealthy New York matron with a fondness for horticulture—was female. The entries came from amateur designers like Parish and from a host of professional designers, including landscape gardeners, architects, and engineers. For almost a month, the members of the Board of Commissioners pondered the merits and shortcomings of the nearly three dozen proposals.

While the 11-man jury deliberated, the question of what New York City's new public park should look like attracted a great deal of attention in the local press. The editor of the *New York Daily Times* wanted Central Park to cater to upper-class New Yorkers by providing spacious carriage drives and a lengthy trotting course for horse fanciers. The city's teeming masses, one *Times* editorial went so far as to declare, should be barred altogether from the expensive new park: "As long as we are governed by the Five Points [a notorious Lower Manhattan slum], our best attempts at elegance and grace will bear some resemblance to jewels in the snouts of swine. Rather the Park should never be made at all if it is to become the resort of rapscalians." In sharp contrast to the *Times*'s class snobbery, *Frank Leslie's Illustrated Newspaper*, a popular working-class journal, urged the Board of Commissioners not to "allocate aristocratic pride and exclusiveness a place where they may strut and parade in a solitary state, but [to create] a spot for all classes of our fellow citizens." Instead of filling the new park with carriage and trotting drives for the benefit of an elite few, planners should focus their efforts on clearing a vast open space where the "laboring classes" could enjoy "café concerts, cirques [circuses], ambulatory [tumbling] exhibitions, and shooting galleries," *Leslie's* declared. The editors of the *Irish News* concurred; they called for the creation of a spacious "public diversion ground" for festivals, fireworks, games, circuses, and other popular working-class amusements.

The newspaper battle over just what the new park should contain and which group—or groups—of New Yorkers it should cater to appears to have had little impact on the park commissioners, however. The 11 board members had their own ideas regarding the appropriate purpose and character of New York's first big public green space. On April 28, 1858, the commissioners made those views clear when they awarded first prize in the design contest to the very last plan to be entered—number 33, dubbed "Greensward" by its anonymous authors.

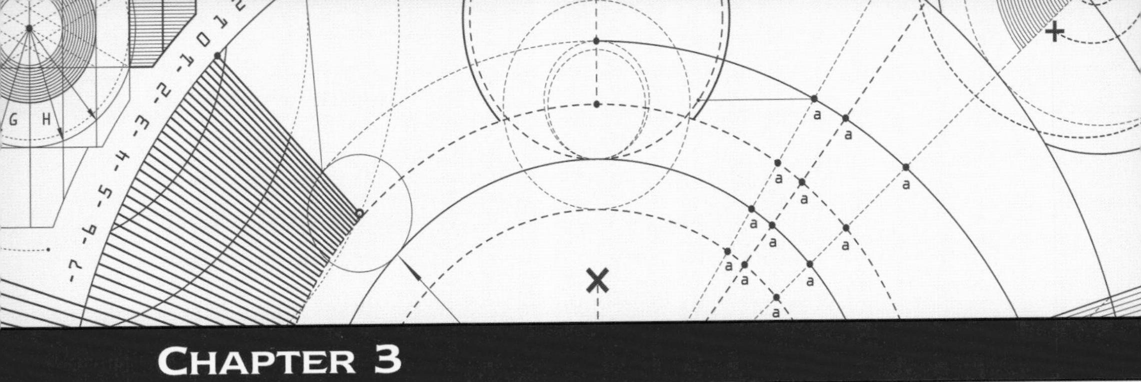

CHAPTER 3

The Greensward Plan

Most scholars agree that the Greensward Plan, the design scheme that the Board of Commissioners of the Central Park ultimately chose for New York's mammoth new public space in April 1858, was nothing less than brilliant. Ambitious and original, yet at the same time remarkably efficient, the Greensward Plan quickly became the standard by which public parks in the United States would be evaluated.

The anonymous authors of the award-winning plan turned out to be none other than Calvert Vaux, the same person who had come up with the idea for a public competition in the first place, and Frederick Law Olmsted, the recently hired superintendent of labor for Central Park. That Vaux—a trained architect and former associate of America's leading landscape gardener, Andrew Jackson Downing—had a hand in the winning entry was hardly surprising. Yet the idea that Vaux's partner in the competition was 36-year-old Frederick Olmsted—a onetime magazine publisher, writer, and gentleman farmer who had never designed anything before in his life—was certainly unexpected.

FREDERICK LAW OLMSTED

Central Park's codesigner had spent much of his young adulthood trying to find his calling. Olmsted, the son of a prosperous Connecticut merchant, had once hoped to study at Yale. After a serious case of sumac poisoning weakened his eyesight, however, he was forced to give up his dream of attending college. In 1843, Olmsted signed up as a deckhand on a merchant ship bound for China, but a bout with scurvy soon convinced the 21-year-old to abandon sailing for farming. After Olmsted spent several frustrating years trying to earn a profit from an experimental scientific farm his father had purchased for him on Staten Island, New York, Olmsted next decided to try his hand at writing. His first book, *Walks and Talks of an American Farmer in England*—a lively account of his travels through Great Britain in 1850—brought him to the attention of the editor of the *New York Daily Times*, Henry J. Raymond. Raymond hired Olmsted to write a series of reports on the slave economy and culture of the American South. Eventually, Olmsted's insightful articles on the pre–Civil War South were compiled and published in two volumes as *The Cotton Kingdom*.

In 1855, at the age of 33, Olmsted embarked on yet another career, this time as a publisher, when he became managing editor of *Putnam's Magazine*. Two years later, the magazine was foundering and Olmsted was on the verge of bankruptcy. Around this time, Central Park commissioner Charles Elliott, an old family friend, encouraged Olmsted to apply for the recently created position of superintendent of labor of New York's new public park. Olmsted required little convincing: He had become a fervent supporter of public parks during his travels in England, where he was particularly impressed by Birkenhead Park, or the "People's Garden," as he called it. Moreover, he was in desperate need of a regular paycheck. Although Olmsted had no supervisory experience to speak of, thanks to the recommendations he received from such influential friends as William Cullen Bryant and Washington Irving, he got the position.

FREDERICK LAW OLMSTED AND *THE COTTON KINGDOM*

To this day, Frederick Law Olmsted (1822–1903) is the most famous landscape architect in U.S. history. He helped design not only Manhattan's Central Park but also an impressive assortment of other celebrated public and private green spaces, including Brooklyn's Prospect Park (1865–1879), Montreal's Mount Royal Park (1874–1881), the U.S. Capitol grounds (1874–1891), and George Vanderbilt's Biltmore Estate in Asheville, North Carolina (1888–1895). Yet, writes Elizabeth Stevenson in *Park Maker: A Life of Frederick Law Olmsted,* "If he had done nothing of note after the 1850s, if there had been no parks, if he had declined into worthy obscurity, Olmsted would still have a secure place in American memory." History would remember Olmsted, Stevenson maintained, as the author of *The Cotton Kingdom*, one of the most vivid and widely read accounts of Southern slaveholding society during the years that immediately preceded the Civil War (1861–1865).

The Cotton Kingdom, originally published in 1861, was based on a series of articles that Olmsted had composed on the South for the *New York Daily Times*. During the first half of the 1850s, Olmsted traveled extensively through the region as a special correspondent for the *Times*. His assignment was to report on how slavery had shaped the South's economy and culture for better or worse.

Still in print today, *The Cotton Kingdom* is an insightful and persuasive condemnation of the South's "peculiar institution." In the book, Olmsted argued that slavery was not only morally repugnant but also economically inefficient. Because of its profit incentives, he maintained, free labor consistently produced higher-quality work, higher output, and higher profits than slave labor. In addition to sapping the South's economic vitality, Olmsted further insisted, slavery had kept the region politically backward. As a consequence of the slaveholding aristocracy's obsession with protecting their way of life, he pointed out, both blacks and whites in the South lacked the freedom of speech that was essential for a true democracy.

Olmsted had been on the job only a few weeks when Vaux asked him to be his partner in the newly announced design competition. Vaux did not seem particularly concerned about the park supervisor's complete lack of design experience. As Vaux later recalled, he was drawn to Olmsted for two reasons. First, because "Olmsted's days were spent on the park territory," Vaux reasoned, he was certain to be intimately familiar with its topography (physical features). Second, Vaux was greatly impressed by Olmsted's *Walks and Talks of an American Farmer in England*, and particularly by its glowing account of Birkenhead Park, which Vaux also admired. Like Olmsted, Vaux believed that a well-designed park could have a positive impact on modern, industrialized society by bringing the serenity of the countryside to overcrowded and overworked city dwellers. By allowing urbanites to escape the noise, throngs, and competitive pressures of the city and immerse themselves in nature—if only for a few hours—a public park could serve as "an educative and civilizing agency," Olmsted wrote, "standing in winning competition against the sordid and corrupting temptations of the town."

THE PARTNERSHIP OF CALVERT VAUX AND FREDERICK OLMSTED

Despite what Olmsted once referred to as his "special instinctive passion" for parks, he was at first hesitant to accept Vaux's invitation to collaborate on the Central Park design. Olmsted's immediate supervisor at the park was Chief Engineer Egbert Viele, whose design plan Vaux had blasted for lacking an "artistic conception." Consequently, Olmsted was wary of associating himself too closely with Vaux. Yet, Olmsted's strong desire to be part of what he viewed as a vitally important project soon won out over his concerns about offending his boss, and—by November 1857—Central Park's new superintendent of labor was devoting most of his free time to the competition.

Because both Olmsted and Vaux always emphasized that their entry was a joint effort, it is impossible to know precisely

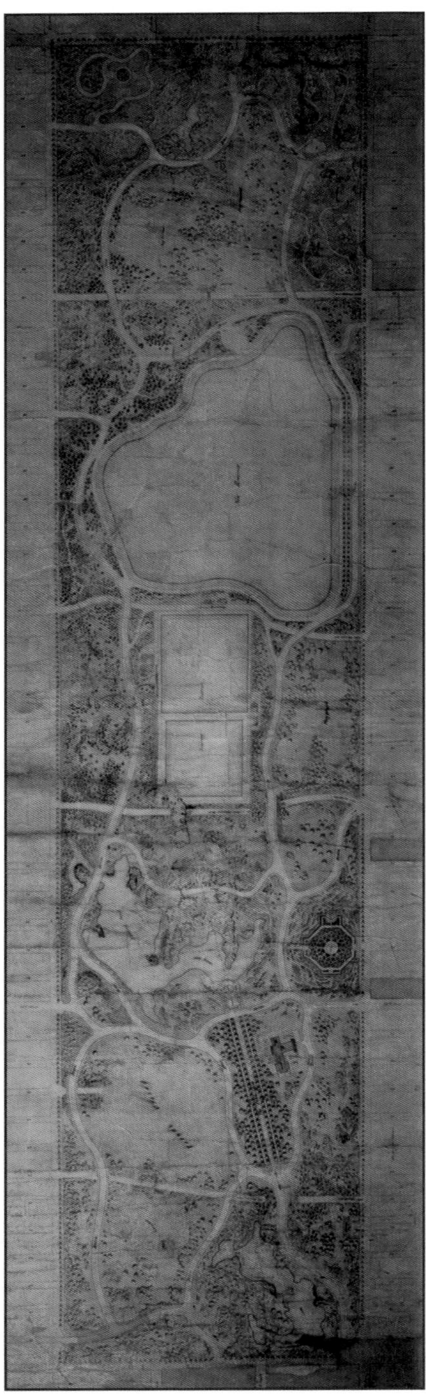

what each man contributed to the Greensward Plan. Yet, it seems likely that neither one could have come up with the celebrated design scheme entirely on his own. In her biography of Frederick Law Olmsted, Elizabeth Stevenson writes regarding the partnership of the young architect and the onetime gentleman farmer: "One supplemented the other. Vaux was more highly trained, and his friend deferred in that technical training; but Olmsted had his useful, rough-and-ready surveyor's skills and was daily on the ground, ranging the park's gaunt, curvy surfaces, imprinting on his mind every hollow in the rocks, every broad space, every ledge."

Created by Calvert Vaux and Frederick Law Olmsted, the winning design for Central Park *(above)* featured a complex network of pedestrian, carriage, and equestrian paths. The designers did not include the formal gardens and ornate statutes typically found in the grand public parks of Paris, London, and other European cities. Instead they strove to create a more natural landscape featuring rolling meadows and lush woodlands.

Throughout the winter of 1857 and 1858, Olmsted and Vaux worked together closely on their plan, formulating and reformulating their ideas. Above all, the men strove to give their scheme what they believed Viele's design lacked: a unifying "artistic conception." For Olmsted and Vaux, Central Park's overarching artistic—and social—purpose was simple: to provide harried, nature-starved New Yorkers with an interlude of "rural" tranquility in the heart of the city. Instead of filling the park with formal gardens and stately monuments and statues, as many of the other competition entries called for, Olmsted and Vaux's naturalistic design stressed meandering paths, woodsy hideaways, and lush, rolling meadows. "The Park," Olmsted explained, "should . . . as far as practicable, resemble a charming bit of rural landscape, such as, unless produced by art, is never found within the limits of a large town."

According to Jeffrey Simpson in *Art of the Olmsted Landscape: His Works in New York City*, Olmsted and Vaux's design for Central Park "was modeled after romantic landscape architecture, which first became popular in eighteenth-century England. In this style meadows and gently undulating [rolling] wooded slopes are varied with lakes and occasionally, 'picturesque' ravines and rocky hills." When it is used to refer to a type of landscape, the word *picturesque* means scenery that has an air of the mysterious and untamed. Roughness, lack of symmetry, and variety are among it chief characteristics.

THE GREENSWARD PLAN: RE-CREATING THE RURAL EXPERIENCE IN THE CITY

It is evident from their Greensward Plan that Olmsted and Vaux placed great importance on moving park visitors out of their dreary urban surroundings and into the park's romantic "rural" environment as quickly as possible. Central Park's primary entrance was to be situated at the southeastern corner of the long narrow rectangle of land, near the bustling intersection of Fifth Avenue and 59th Street. To shift visitors' attention away from the noisy thoroughfares and drab buildings that bordered the entrance, Olmsted and Vaux had the main drive into the park run diagonally into the center of the half-mile-wide site.

The interior of the rock-strewn, largely barren southern (or lower) park, however, was a far cry from the verdant rural landscape of Olmsted and Vaux's imaginings. Meadowland, an essential component of the rural experience that the two designers hoped to re-create on the park site, was almost nonexistent in the lower park. To create the lush meadowland necessary for their bucolic vision, Olmsted and Vaux proposed blasting, filling, and seeding the rocky, uneven terrain on the lower park's western side. The northern portion of this broad, grassy plain was to serve as the park's mandated parade ground. On the lower park's swampy eastern side, Vaux and Olmsted planned to take advantage of the existing landscape by creating a large pond picturesquely bordered by bold rock bluffs.

The most prominent design feature of the lower park in the Greensward Plan was also one of the naturalistic scheme's few formal elements: a quarter-mile-long promenade or mall—a broad, gravel-lined avenue flanked by double rows of regularly spaced American elm trees. "Although averse [disinclined] on general principles to a symmetrical arrangement of trees," wrote Olmsted and Vaux in the description that accompanied their plan, "we consider it an essential feature of a metropolitan park, that it should contain a grand promenade."

The two designers did not envision their elm-lined avenue as merely an elegant spot for the fashionable to see and be seen, as many of their contemporaries might have supposed. Rather, Olmsted and Vaux wanted the mall to be a democratic public space, where New Yorkers from different economic and social classes could meet and mingle. New Yorkers "display a remarkable quickness of apprehension [along with] a peculiarly hard sort of selfishness," Olmsted contended. "Every day of their

After trying his hand at farming, sailing, and journalism, Frederick Law Olmsted *(above)* decided to apply for a position at the New York City parks department. As Superintendent of Labor, Olmsted used his knowledge in horticulture, agriculture, and landscaping to help Calvert Vaux design one of the most famous parks in the world.

lives they have seen thousands of their fellow-men . . . have brushed against them, and yet have had no experience of anything in common with them. There need to be places and times for re-unions [where] the rich and poor, the cultivated and the self-made, shall be attracted together and encouraged to assimilate."

VISTA ROCK AND THE UPPER PARK

Directly to the east of the mall, Olmsted and Vaux planned to introduce two more formal elements to the park—the music hall and the large garden that were required by the competition's

BUILDING AMERICA NOW

MILLENNIUM PARK: CHICAGO'S GRAND NEW PUBLIC SPACE

On July 16, 2004, Chicago's Millennium Park officially opened amid enormous popular and critical acclaim. Despite its choice location in the heart of downtown Chicago along Lake Michigan, the Millennium Park site had been an unsightly railroad yard for more than a century and a half. When the land finally became available in the late 1990s, Mayor Richard M. Daley jumped at the chance to create a grand new public space for the Windy City next to spacious Grant Park, Chicago's so-called "front yard" since its construction in the early twentieth century.

Millennium Park, which covers 24.5 acres, is a fraction of the size of Central Park. Nonetheless, Chicago's striking new public space has already become not only a major tourist destination but also a symbol for the Windy City in much the same way that Central Park is one of New York City's most famous icons. For six years, urban planners, landscape designers, artists, and architects united to create the most rules. At the head of the mall, the two designers placed a big fountain (another required element) and a graceful water terrace (later dubbed Bethesda Terrace) that led down to a man-made lake, identified simply as "the Lake" in the Greensward Plan. In keeping with their fundamental artistic conception of the park as a rural environment, however, Olmsted and Vaux pointed their elegant terrace and mall at what the men considered as the most impressive natural feature of the entire park site: craggy Vista Rock. Located on the northernmost fringes of the lower park, the rugged, heavily wooded bluff stood directly across the lake from their proposed mall and terrace. Consequently, as visitors

ambitious public project in Chicago history—a combined outdoor art museum, cultural center, and landscaped park. The cost of this mammoth undertaking was $475 million—when adjusted for inflation, nearly twice what it cost to build Central Park between 1858 and 1877. Owing to an unprecedented partnership between Chicago's government and the philanthropic community, however, approximately half of the park's funding came from private donors that included individuals and families, nonprofit organizations, and business corporations.

The Millennium project's remarkable success in attracting private funds rested largely on its founders' ability to persuade world-renowned designers and artists, such as architect Frank Gehry, sculptors Jaume Plensa and Anish Kapoor, and landscape architect Kathryn Gustafson, to help create the park's numerous "enhancements." Among the most popular of Millennium Park's various amenities since its opening in 2004 are the Jay Pritzker Pavilion, Gehry's dazzling stainless-steel band shell; Plensa's high-tech Crown Fountain; Kapoor's massive, interactive sculpture, *Cloud Gate*; and Gustafson's dramatic and graceful Lurie Garden.

passed along the mall and terrace, note Charles E. Beveridge and Paul Rocheleau in *Frederick Law Olmsted: Designing the American Landscape*, "the central focus of their vision was not a statue or an artificial object, but instead the green hillside of Vista Rock itself." On the southern side of the bluff, Olmsted and Vaux planned to create a romanticized miniature forest, complete with picturesque man-made streams and waterfalls, winding footpaths, and a *grotto*, or cave. In time, this section of Vista Rock would come to be known as the Ramble.

Just beyond steep Vista Rock, on the northern or upper portion of the park, lurked what most people agreed was a major eyesore: a large, rectangular municipal reservoir—a receiving pool for clean water from the dammed-up Croton River, approximately 40 miles north of New York City. (In 1862, an even larger, irregularly shaped reservoir, which since 1994 has been known as the Jacqueline Kennedy Onassis Reservoir, was constructed just to the rectangular reservoir's north, covering most of the park's width between 86th and 96th streets.) So that the unattractive receiving pool would not mar the scenic rural experience Olmsted and Vaux were striving to create, the designers urged that a thick border of trees and tall shrubs be planted around it.

The Greensward Plan called for relatively few alterations to the land north of the reservoirs, which constituted the heart of the upper park. In sharp contrast to the barren, rocky terrain of the lower park, much of the northern portion of the Central Park site consisted of gently rolling grassland. Olmsted and Vaux wanted this broad, open plain, which would eventually be named the North and East Meadows, to remain as wild as possible. Between the vast plains of the upper park and the spacious grasslands that Olmsted and Vaux proposed to create in the southwestern portion of the park, the Greensward Plan contained more acres of meadowland than any of the other Central Park competition entries. When the two designers chose their proposal's name, they clearly wanted to call attention to this distinguishing characteristic of their plan—the word *greensward* means unbroken stretches of grassy turf.

AN INGENIOUS TRAFFIC CIRCULATION SYSTEM

The Greensward Plan stood out from the other competition entries for New York's grand new public park not only because of the large amount of meadowland that it included, but also because of the ingenious way in which Olmsted and Vaux handled the site's traffic circulation system. According to the rules of the design contest, every entry had to include at least four east-west public roads to accommodate crosstown traffic. Yet Olmsted and Vaux hated the idea of allowing noisy and "coarse" city traffic to mar the beautiful and serene rural landscape they hoped to create, as the designers explained at length in their "Description of a Plan for the Improvement of the Central Park: 'Greensward'":

> Each of [the required transverse roads] will be the sole line of communication between one side of town and the other. . . . Inevitably they will be crowded thoroughfares, having nothing in common with the park proper, but everything at variance with those agreeable sentiments which we would wish the park to inspire. . . . They must be constantly open to all the legitimate traffic of the city, to coal carts and butchers' carts, dust carts and dung carts; [fire] engine companies will use them, those on one side of the park rushing their machines across it with frantic zeal at every alarm from the other; ladies and invalids will need special police escort for crossing them . . . ; eight times in a single circuit of the park will they oblige a pleasure drive or stroll to encounter a turbid stream of coarse traffic, constantly moving at right angles to the line of the park movement.

To address this problem, Olmsted and Vaux proposed something that no other entrant in the design competition had thought of: They suggested installing all four of the obligatory transverse roads in large, excavated trenches, several feet below the park's surface. To conceal the sunken thoroughfares from the view of

On the southern side of the craggy bluff known as Vista Rock, Olmsted and Vaux designed the Ramble, a lush miniature forest with meandering footpaths, sparkling waterfalls, and a picturesque man-made grotto. Known for its wide variety of trees and other plants, this section of the park is also frequented by birdwatchers hoping to catch a glimpse of one of 270 species that have been spotted there.

park visitors and to minimize traffic noise, they recommended that tall fences and thick plantings of trees and shrubs be placed along their borders. Scholars agree that Olmsted and Vaux's scheme for locating the transverse roads below ground level was as efficient as it was inventive. The submerged public thoroughfares not only would help to keep the distracting sights and sounds of the city from intruding on park visitors' "rural" experience, they also would allow Manhattan's increasing crosstown traffic to move through the park at a more rapid rate because it would not mix with slow-moving "pleasure" traffic.

Shortly after Olmsted and Vaux won the design competition in late April 1858, they expanded this innovative separation to include Central Park's interior circulation system, using an idea borrowed from the second-place winner in the contest, Samuel Gustin. So that visitors could give their full attention to the rustic scenery without having to worry about colliding with others using a different form of transportation, Olmsted and Vaux created three distinct circulation systems within the park: walkways for pedestrians, broad drives for carriages, and bridle paths for horseback riders. The two designers planned to achieve this division of functions by placing bridges or arched passageways wherever the various equestrian paths, carriage drives, and footways intersected within the park.

Olmsted and Vaux's naturalistic yet remarkably efficient design clearly set the Greensward Plan apart from its competitors in the minds of the commissioners who awarded them first prize. Yet, as the park board soon discovered, turning the designers' vision of a beautiful rural retreat in the middle of Manhattan into reality would be an enormously costly, lengthy, and labor-intensive undertaking.

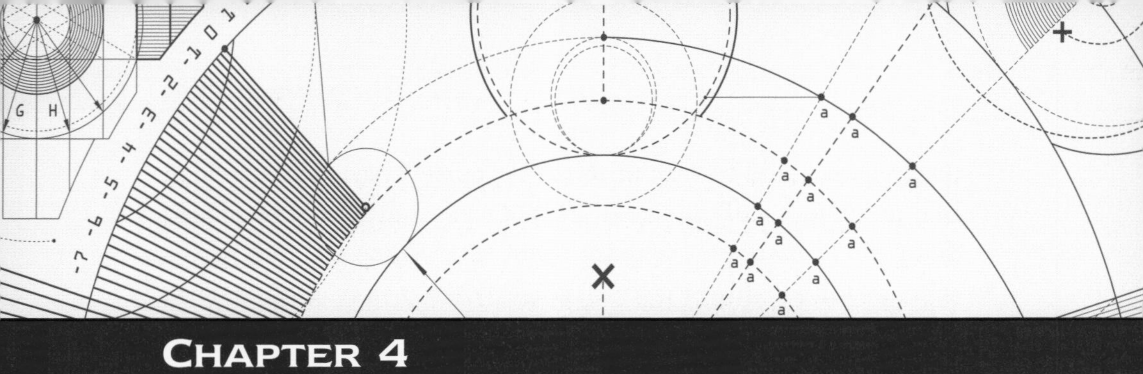

CHAPTER 4

Clearing, Draining, and Dredging

Building Central Park according to Frederick Law Olmsted and Calvert Vaux's ambitious landscaping design was an extremely time-consuming and arduous process. To create the beautiful "natural" scenery that the two designers described in their Greensward Plan, workers would eventually have to remodel virtually every inch of the rocky, swampy site. As Olmsted would later observe, "It would have been difficult to find another body of land of seven hundred acres upon the island . . . which possessed less of . . . the most desirable characteristics of a park, or upon which more time, labor and expense would be required to establish them."

CLEARING THE PARK SITE

Clearing of the Central Park site actually began long before the Board of Commissioners awarded first prize to Olmsted and Vaux's Greensward design in April 1858. Late in the summer of 1857, approximately 500 workers hired by Chief Engineer Egbert Viele started the demanding job of stripping the soggy, boulder-strewn land below the big municipal reservoir at 79th Street. Toiling 10 hours a day, 6 days a week under the blazing August sun, gangs of 15 to 20 men each tore down abandoned cottages, churches, stables, and workshops; dismantled stone walls; and cleared out pig yards.

Other work crews, equipped only with shovels and pick-axes, dug up hundreds of small boulders and loaded them onto horse-drawn carts for transportation to the park's periphery, where muscular "stone breakers" used sledgehammers to pound the rocks into 2- to 6-inch paving stones for roadways. More than two years after work commenced on the site, the park's construction workers were finally freed of this back-breaking and extremely time-consuming task by mechanized stone crushers. Patented in 1858 by Eli Whitney Blake—the nephew of the famous inventor of the cotton gin, Eli Whitney—the mechanized crushers used by the park construction crews consisted of a pair of upright jaws, one movable and one stationary. Workers simply fed rocks into the big steel jaws; when they closed, the stones would be pulverized to the desired size.

THE DETESTED JOB OF "GRUBBING"

One of the most hated jobs during the early weeks and months of clearing the park was "grubbing," removing the thick and often noxious underbrush that surrounded the plot's foul-smelling swamps. "Grubbers" made every effort to avoid contact between their uncovered skin and the poison ivy and sumac that flourished near the park's many bogs and marshes. One grubbing gang made a critical mistake, however, when they decided to dispose of the uprooted vines and shrubs by burning them on a huge bonfire. What the men did not realize is that burning poison ivy or sumac can release microscopic droplets of the plants' toxic oils into the air. Many of the unwitting grubbers suffered painful rashes in their nasal passages and throats when they inhaled oil-laden smoke from the burning plants, and a few became seriously

One of the largest public works projects in the history of New York City began months before a design was even chosen for the park. Because the designated site was unfit for park construction, workers were hired to tear down houses and walls, blast through rock, and haul away debris *(above)*. The work was difficult and dangerous, and the laborers were susceptible to disease and allergic reactions.

ill after they developed allergic rashes to the oil in their bronchial tubes or lungs, a condition that is potentially fatal.

Coming into contact with the noxious oils of the poison ivy and sumac plants was not the only occupational hazard associated with grubbing. The men assigned to clear the park's bug-infested wetlands were also at high risk of contracting a grave and often deadly infectious disease: malaria. Malaria, or "ague" as the illness was commonly known in the nineteenth century, is characterized by recurrent bouts of fever, chills, and sweating. In ancient times, people realized that malarial outbreaks and wetlands were somehow connected. It was not until the early twentieth century, however, that researchers uncovered the disease's true cause: a protozoan parasite that is transmitted to humans by the bite of an infected mosquito. Late in the summer of 1857, several grubbers toiling near an ideal mosquito breeding ground—a particularly large bog described by one observer as "filled with mud and filthy yellow water"—came down with malaria. By the beginning of October, Central Park's brand-new superintendent of labor, Frederick Law Olmsted, reported that nearly one in seven of the park's grubbers had "been attacked with intermittent fever during the past fortnight [two weeks]."

"WE WANT WORK"

Clearing the rugged Central Park site was grueling and sometimes hazardous work, and the pay—at just 10 cents an hour—was low. Nonetheless, during the late summer and fall of 1857, tens of thousands of New Yorkers sought employment at the city's huge new public works project. At the time, Manhattan, along with much of the rest of the nation, was in the grips of a major economic downturn. Unemployment was rampant on the island, particularly among the unskilled laborers who formed the bulk of New York City's population, and in desperation many laid-off laborers took to the streets. Protesters rallied by the thousands at City Hall, in Tompkins Square, and in Central Park

CENTRAL PARK'S OLDEST MAN-MADE OBJECT: THE OBELISK

By far the oldest man-made object in Central Park is the imposing 71-foot-tall obelisk located on Greywacke Knoll directly behind the Metropolitan Museum of Art. Obelisks—also called "needles"—are narrow, four-sided stone monuments with pointed or pyramidal tops that were placed in pairs before the entrances to ancient Egyptian temples. Presented to the United States by the Egyptian government in 1879, Central Park's towering red granite pillar dates to about 1450 B.C., when it was first erected in the Egyptian city of On, or Heliopolis, by Pharaoh Thothmes III. Although the obelisk was popularly dubbed Cleopatra's Needle, it was created nearly 15 centuries before the legendary Egyptian queen's birth.

Transporting the 244-ton obelisk from Alexandria, Egypt (where it had been moved from Heliopolis during the first century B.C.), to Central Park was a very expensive and delicate undertaking. Financed by American railroad tycoon William Vanderbilt, the journey took nearly six months and cost more than $100,000. In July 1880, after a 38-day ocean voyage, the obelisk was finally unloaded at the 51st Street dock on the Hudson River and hoisted onto a specially reinforced cart. The obelisk's slow, arduous journey over a specially built wooden trestle from the waterfront to its final resting spot on Greywacke Knoll, north of the Ramble on the park's eastern edge, took well over 100 days.

When the obelisk was finally turned upright on January 22, 1881, an estimated 20,000 New Yorkers descended on Central Park for the festive raising ceremony. Seventy-five years later, the famous Hollywood movie director Cecil B. DeMille—who had many fond memories of playing in Central Park as a child—donated the funds for a plaque at the obelisk's base that translated into English the hieroglyphics covering much of the monument. The obelisk's hieroglyphics describe the accomplishments of Thothmes III and of another Egyptian pharaoh, Ramses II, who lived about two centuries later.

itself, where they picketed the headquarters of the new superintendent of labor. Day after day, Olmsted would arrive at work to find his office surrounded by as many as 5,000 angry demonstrators carrying muslin banners inscribed with such slogans as "We Want Work" and the more ominous "Bread or Blood." At one point, Olmsted later recalled, the protesters "sent in to me a list of 10,000 names of men alleged to have starving families, demanding that they should be immediately put to work."

When the Board of Commissioners finally granted Olmsted permission to hire 1,000 additional men in early November 1857, he was inundated with applications. Yet, the fortunate few who were awarded park jobs that autumn had little hope of holding onto them for long. Resolved to stretch the coveted positions as far as they possibly could, during Olmsted's first fall and winter with Central Park the commissioners relied heavily on the tactic of rotated employment. "We unexpectedly received an order to pay off and discharge all men this week, and have been doing it," Olmsted complained in a letter to his father in late 1857 regarding his continually changing workforce. Next week, he predicted, "we shall probably take on an even larger force."

Despite his frustration with the frequent turnover in his workforce, Olmsted derived great satisfaction from his new supervisory role. Years later, Olmsted would remember his early days at Central Park as an exhilarating battle of wills in which he molded "a mob of lazy, reckless, turbulent and violent loafers" into a "well-organized, punctual, sober, industrious and disciplined body." From the start, Olmsted made a point to closely monitor his employees' work time. According to his stringent absentee rules, if a laborer missed just two days of work, he risked immediate dismissal. When Olmsted discovered that some workers were getting around his strict new requirements by having a buddy answer "present" for them during the twice-daily roll calls, he introduced a military-style attendance drill. First thing in the morning and directly after lunch, a bell signaled the men to line up according to their assigned work gangs. When

Olmsted and Vaux designed transverse roads across Central Park to allow a steady flow of crosstown traffic. In order to shield the signs of urban life from park visitors, the roads were built below the level of the park grounds. *Above*, a cluster of small cottages housing the park's original inhabitants sits behind a construction site for one of the transverse roads in Central Park.

a man's name was called, he took two steps forward. Foremen were ordered to look the man directly in the eye and confirm that the name and the face matched. Fairly or not, Olmsted—who once characterized the park's largely immigrant workforce as representatives of "the poorest or what is generally considered the most dangerous class of the great city's population"—seems to have had little faith in his laborers' fundamental integrity.

THE MEN WHO BUILT CENTRAL PARK

The park workforce included a variety of skilled artisans, such as carpenters, stonemasons, and blacksmiths, who repaired broken carts and tools. Yet, the vast majority of the men who built Central Park were unskilled laborers. More than three-quarters of the laborers were first- and second-generation Irish, and a significant portion of the rest were German immigrants. Not a single black man labored on the park's construction gangs. During a period of widespread racial prejudice in the northern United States, when white laborers often protested the hiring of African Americans by walking off their jobs, the park board was clearly determined to avoid any trouble. Traditional attitudes toward occupational segregation also kept women off the park's construction force. Central Park's sole female employees during its first years of operation were washroom attendants or office cleaners.

The unskilled laborers who made up the bulk of Central Park's construction force typically toiled from 6:00 A.M. until 5:00 P.M., with an hour off for lunch, Monday through Saturday, and they did all this for the relatively low wage of 50 cents to one dollar a day. The work was backbreaking—one contractor claimed that "he had never worked a gang of men so hard on any contract as he had done on the park"—and the pay skimpy, but Central Park's thousands of construction positions offered steady employment during a period when joblessness was rampant among Manhattan's lower classes. Moreover, for a handful of workers, the possibility existed of being promoted into the higher-paying and less arduous positions of assistant foreman or foreman.

Decades after Central Park opened, a descendent of several Irish laborers who helped construct it complained that the contributions of the city's poor to the creation of the great public space had been largely forgotten in accounts of the park by scholars and other middle- or upper-class writers. In a *Daily News* article, the man, referred to only as a "Bronx Old Timer," mused: "I wonder if any of these artists, landscape architects, or philanthropists . . . know how the poor of New York built Central Park. When my parents used to take me to the park as a child, my father used to tell us how my grandfather and great uncles had worked on the park job at 50 cents a day. . . . The park area was given to the city in the first place by a few wealthy men to make work for the poor. And it was understood that the poor were to enjoy the park."

DRAINING AND DREDGING

Six months after Olmsted assumed his duties as superintendent of labor for Central Park and just two weeks after the Greensward Plan won first prize in the design competition, the commissioners dismissed Chief Engineer Viele and gave Olmsted an impressive new title—architect in chief. Calvert Vaux was named as Olmsted's assistant, even though the men had always claimed equal responsibility for the winning design, and Vaux was the one with the formal architectural training. Vaux,

BUILDING AMERICA NOW

PALEY PARK: MANHATTAN'S MOST POPULAR "POCKET PARK"

Pocket parks, also known as vest-pocket parks, are very small open spaces that are typically built in urban areas. As available land for urban parks has become ever scarcer and costlier in recent decades, pocket parks have sprung up in a number of America's larger cities, including New York. The best known and most popular of New York City's various pocket parks is Paley Park on East 53th Street, a short distance southeast of Central Park.

Funded by the founder of the Columbia Broadcasting System, William S. Paley (1901–1990), as a memorial to his late father, Paley Park was built on the site of a demolished seven-story building. Measuring just 4,200 square feet, or .10 acres, the famous pocket park is less than 1/800 of the size of nearby Central Park. Construction on the tiny public space began in the winter of 1966, and the park officially however, accepted the commissioners' decision with good grace. The architect in chief's responsibilities included hiring and overseeing the park's construction workers and police force; in sharp contrast to Olmsted, Vaux heartily disliked organizational and managerial tasks.

Olmsted's first challenge as architect in chief of Central Park was to oversee one of the most crucial steps in the entire construction process: draining the park's soggy ground. An effective drainage system was considered of vital importance to the new park for many reasons. First, such a system was necessary to keep park walkways—and visitors' feet—dry. Second, it was critical for sustaining the rich, loose subsoil required to support the hundreds of thousands of trees, shrubs, and other plants that

opened a year and a half later. The project's cost, including purchase of the land, was approximately $1 million. In 1999, a little more than three decades after Paley Park's creation, the William S. Paley Foundation spent $700,000 to have the park completely reconstructed according to its original design.

Designed with adults in mind—particularly office workers, tourists, and shoppers looking for a respite from the noise and crowds of busy midtown Manhattan—Paley Park has tables and chairs and a small concession stand but no playground equipment. Seventeen honey locust trees were planted throughout the site, and a 20-foot waterfall was constructed along the park's entire back wall. The thundering cascade provides a stunning focal point for the park while also helping to drown out the sounds of the city. According to one estimate, Paley Park attracts at least 500,000 visits per year—far less than the 25 million people who visit Central Park annually but an impressive number for a park that is just one-tenth of an acre in size.

Olmsted and Vaux planned to put in throughout the site. Only poison sumac, skunk cabbage, and other undesirable plants could flourish in the park's typically waterlogged flats, the new architect in chief declared in his first report to the commissioners on drainage, and during droughts the site's dense, clay-based soil would harden and "interpose a hydraulic floor between the thirsty roots in the surface soil and the moisture of the cool earth below." Last, but not least, everyone agreed that the park needed to be thoroughly drained for health reasons. The close link between malaria and marshland was well established by the mid-nineteenth century, even if the actual cause of the disease was not yet understood. In a report on Central Park penned in 1856, Chief Engineer Viele warned that, unless the site was thoroughly drained, it would remain a "pestilential [noxious] spot, where rank vegetation and miasmatic [poisonous] odors taint every breath of air."

Early in the summer of 1858, Olmsted placed a young, talented sanitation engineer by the name of George Edwin Waring in charge of devising and installing a drainage system for Central Park. Waring was also to be responsible for excavating the scenic, man-made lakes and ponds that Olmsted and Vaux had described in their Greensward Plan. Waring's crew of 400 men began to scoop out a series of channels in the southern half of the park to open the area's numerous clogged pools and streams. Central Park would ultimately boast three major bodies of water: the 5-acre pond in the park's southeastern corner, the 22-acre lake at its center, and the 11-acre *meer* (Dutch for "lake") in its northeastern corner.

Next, the 24-year-old sanitation engineer directed his crew to dig 3- to 4-foot-deep trenches at regularly spaced intervals across the lower park. Into these narrow ditches the men placed clay drainage pipes or tiles, which measured between 1.5 and 6 inches in diameter. The carefully fitted pipes drew moisture downward from the park's boggy areas into specially constructed collecting drains. According to Waring's ingenious scheme, the water in the

Above, a view of the Lake, located just south of the Ramble. Hurriedly built to coincide with ice-skating season, the lake was an instant hit with the public. The remaining houses of Central Park's former residents—incorrectly labeled as "squatters" by the media—can be seen in the background.

collecting drains would then be routed through brick sewers to the ponds and lakes that Olmsted and Vaux planned to excavate in the park's lowest areas. Eventually, Waring hoped to place clay drainage pipes under 500 acres of the park site.

By late 1858, Waring's hardworking crews had laid nearly two dozen miles of *subterranean* (underground) drainage pipes. Of considerably more interest to the people of New York City, they had also managed to fill the large 22-acre artificial lake just below scenic Vista Rock that the Greensward Plan called for. Waring's men had accomplished this impressive feat by dredging the huge bog that lay south of Vista Rock to a depth of 7 feet at its center, then directing runoff water from the wooded southern slope of the rock through a series of pipes and into the scooped-out swamp. The Lake, as Central Park's largest body of water was labeled in the Greensward Plan and is still known today, was completed just in time for the ice-skating season; during the winter of 1858–1859, it became the first park attraction to be opened

BUILDING AMERICA NOW

CRISSY FIELD: SAN FRANCISCO'S NEW URBAN OASIS

Crissy Field, which officially opened in 2001, is part of San Francisco's 75,000-acre Golden Gate National Recreation Area, the biggest urban national park in the world. Crissy Field's 100 acres include meadows, marshes, dunes (sandhills), a spacious public beach, and Crissy Field Center, a large outdoor education center. Because Crissy Field was once a U.S. Army airfield, it was constructed almost entirely from private donations (in contrast to the government-funded Central Park). Final costs for the new bayside park totaled more than $34 million but would have been considerably higher if much of the work had not been carried out by several thousand local volunteers.

Crissy Field's scenic "natural" landscape, like that of Central Park, is almost entirely man-made. Between 1997 and the park's completion in 2001, 87,000 tons of asphalt and other debris were hauled away from the obsolete military airfield to make room for a 29-acre meadow. In addition, a 20-acre tidal marsh linked to San Francisco Bay was bulldozed; 22 acres of rippling shoreline dunes were constructed; and 100,000 native plants, including dune grass and beach strawberries, were seeded or planted. The park's extensive, man-made coastal marsh system was intended to replicate the large salt marsh and coastal dunes that covered most of the 100-acre site before they were destroyed by early twentieth-century development. Today the park's restored dunes and marsh furnish a rich habitat—which did not exist in the area for nearly 100 years—for native wildlife, including approximately 20 different fish species and well over 100 bird species.

to the public. Skating had long been a popular sport in New York City, but by the late 1850s few skating ponds were left in the rapidly expanding city. Consequently, Central Park's vast new lake was immediately filled with recreational skaters. Although it would take another 18 years before the rest of Olmsted and Vaux's original Greensward vision would be realized, by early 1859 it was already evident that their pseudo-rural sanctuary in the midst of Manhattan had found a secure place in the hearts of New Yorkers. "New York at length has its crowning triumph," gushed editor George William Curtis in *Harper's Monthly Magazine* in 1859, as work on the new park continued. "It is a garden in the largest and most generous sense—not a series of flower-beds, but a system of avenues, drives, walks, paths, terraces, laws, streams, falls, bridges, grottoes, tunnels, shrubberies, groves, hedges, flowers, and all that human intelligence can achieve in adorning and beautifying the earth."

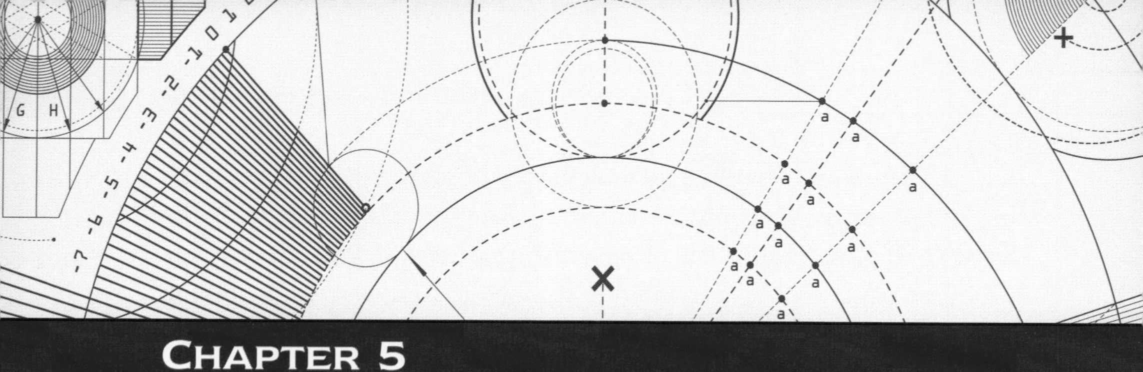

CHAPTER 5

Filling, Blasting, and Planting

Construction on Central Park continued even as thousands of New Yorkers began pouring into their city's vast new public space to skate on the newly completed lake during the winter of 1858–1859. With the jobs of scooping out the park's lakes and ponds and creating its underground drainage system well under way, laborers began to redo the plot's uneven and rocky topography according to Olmsted and Vaux's Greensward Plan. From one end of the long rectangular plot to the other, work crews blasted out ridges and boulders; spread tens of thousands of cartloads of topsoil; seeded dozens of acres of new meadowland; planted more than a quarter of a billion trees, shrubs, and vines; and graded and paved 70 miles of meticulously laid-out carriage drives, bridle paths, and walkways. "Every foot of the park," Olmsted would later declare with obvious pride, "every tree and bush, every arch, roadway and walk, has been fixed where it is *with a purpose*."

FILLING, GRADING, AND PAVING

In addition to the park's drainage engineer, George Edwin Waring, approximately two dozen other engineers contributed their expertise to the construction of Central Park. Their work was supervised by William H. Grant, Egbert Viele's replacement as chief engineer. Grant had helped direct several major public works projects, including the recent enlargement of the Erie Canal. Olmsted—who never hesitated to delegate responsibility to talented subordinates—placed great faith in Grant's judgment.

As soon as Waring's crews had completed the drainage of an area, other work gangs under the supervision of Grant and his four assistant engineers began the daunting task of sculpting the park's natural topography to fit Olmsted and Vaux's bucolic vision. It was a process that required an enormous expenditure of man- and horsepower. Olmsted would later estimate that the amount of soil moved during the building of Central Park, much of which had been imported to the site from Long Island and New Jersey meadowlands, totaled "nearly ten millions of ordinary city one-horse cart loads, which, in single file, would make a procession thirty thousand . . . miles in length." According to Charles Beveridge and Paul Rocheleau in *Frederick Law Olmsted: Designing the American Landscape*, "This was the equivalent to altering the level of the entire surface of the park by four feet."

Once the lower park's pedestrian walks and carriage drives had been graded (leveled or smoothed to a desired gradient or rate of inclination) by Grant's crews, the time-consuming job of paving them began. In *The Park and the People: A History of Central Park*, authors Rosenzweig and Blackmar describe the lengthy process of creating paved roads capable of withstanding upward ground movement from below the frost line that could push rocks to the surface, causing troublesome potholes and ruts:

Laborers manually wedged together rectangular foundation stones to create an even surface at a depth of seven to eight inches. After rolling this substratum [a layer lying under another], they added a five-inch layer of smaller stones supplied by the stone breakers, a layer designed to relieve the foundation from the compacting effect of surface traffic. Special gangs of pavers, paid ten cents a day more than laborers, topped the middle stratum [layer] with a one-and-a-half-inch layer of finely screened gravel (intermixed with moistened loam [a rich soil] and sand as binders), and this was rolled and compacted by a six-and-a-half-ton cylinder pulled by eight horses. At the edges

A CONTEMPORARY ACCOUNT OF CENTRAL PARK UNDER CONSTRUCTION

Late in the spring of 1859, New York City lawyer and diarist George Templeton Strong visited Central Park with his young son and recorded the following observations in his daily journal:

> Improved the day by leaving Wall Street early and set off to explore the Central Park, which will be a feature of the city within five years and a lovely place in A.D. 1900, when its trees will have acquired dignity and appreciable diameters. Perhaps the city itself will perish before then, by growing too big to live under faulty institutions corruptly administered. Reached the park a little before four, just as the red flag was hoisted—the signal for the blasts of the day. They were all around us for some twenty minutes, now booming far off to the north, now quite near, now distant again, like a desultory "affair" between two great armies.

Regarding the wooded Ramble on the southern slope of Vista Rock and the lower park, Strong noted:

road gangs built gutters and laid tiles to keep new drives from flooding.

BLASTING OUT BOULDERS AND RIDGES

Remodeling the lower park according to the Greensward Plan was not only a labor-intensive process, it could also be a very dangerous one. Before the rocky, uneven terrain that made up much of the lower park could be filled with topsoil and graded to create roadbeds, meadows, or the formal mall, its many great boulders and schist outcroppings had to be removed. To accomplish this daunting task, laborers used hammers, pickaxes,

> Its footpaths and plantations [plantings] are finished, more or less, and it is the first section of the ground that has been polished off and made presentable. It promises very well. So does the lower park, though now in most rugged condition: . . ."lakes" without water, mounds of compost, piles of blasted stone, acres of what may be greensward hereafter but is now mere brown earth; groves of slender young transplanted maples and locusts, undecided between life and death, with here and there an arboricultural experiment that has failed utterly and is a mere broomstick with ramifications [offshoots or branches].

Nonetheless, Strong asserted, "the work promised very well. . . . Celts [a reference to the park's many Irish laborers], caravans of dirt carts, . . . [and] steam engines are the elements out of which our future Pleasance [pleasure] is rapidly developing. The work seems pushed with vigor and system, and as far as it has gone, looks thorough and substantial."

shovels, and nearly 170 tons of gunpowder—more than was fired by the Union and Confederate armies at the famed Battle of Gettysburg in 1863. (Central Park's builders did not use dynamite because it had not yet been invented.)

During the first two years of construction, two Irish immigrants, Luke Flynn and Timothy McNamera, were killed by explosions. Over the next several years, three more men would die in blasting accidents in Central Park. Yet, in light of the extensive blasting required to produce level ground for meadows and create the submerged transverse roads, the number of explosion-related injuries was actually quite low. The relatively small number of injuries, historians agree, was a direct consequence of the meticulous safety procedures developed by Olmsted and Grant for their "rock gangs," as the blasting crews were known. For example, foremen of rock gangs were required to give two hours of advance notice before setting a charge. To signal an upcoming blast, a large red flag was raised on the park's tall bell tower. Until that flag was lowered and a white one raised in its place to signal that the blasting was finished, all other work gangs in the general vicinity of the blasting had to stop whatever they were doing and take cover.

PLANTING THE PARK

In October 1858, Olmsted's gardening crew planted their very first tree. "After this," notes Olmsted biographer Elizabeth Stevenson, "the planting never let up." In the course of constructing Central Park according to Olmsted and Vaux's vision of a beautiful rural sanctuary in the city, gardeners put in tens of thousands of trees and millions of shrubs, vines, and other plants. The bulk of this massive planting was supervised by Ignaz Anton Pilat, a highly trained Austrian gardener. After Pilat completed his studies of botany at the University of Vienna, he served as assistant director of Vienna's Imperial Botanical Gardens before he emigrated to the United States in 1848. When Olmsted appointed him as chief gardener of Central Park in 1861, the German-speaking

Olmsted planted millions of trees, shrubs, vines, and other plants, mostly along the park's perimeter. Aside from using thick plantings of trees and shrubs along the park's borders as a natural barrier against the city's noise and congestion, Olmsted hoped to make Central Park into one of the world's leading arboretums. To that end, he had more than 300 different species of trees planted on the park's grounds.

Pilat quickly attained the loyalty and respect of the park's gardening crews, which were largely composed of recent German immigrants.

Much of the early planting of Central Park was focused on the park's perimeters. To ensure that visitors to their pseudo-rural retreat could escape as completely as possible from the city's noise and congestion, Olmsted and Vaux tried to shut out the surrounding urban environment by planting a thick barrier of shrubs and trees along the park's borders. An added benefit of these perimeter plantings was that they helped to obscure the park's elongated shoebox shape, which made the narrow plot appear wider than it actually was.

Olmsted also strove to create artistic compositions with his plantings by carefully arranging them according to their varying textures, shapes, and colors. "Writing to his gardeners," observes author Sara Cedar Miller,

> Olmsted communicated his aesthetic vision in the same way that a painter would instruct his studio assistants: "In [the Ramble woodlands] the surface should be more or less rough and rude, the trees and shrubs should grow in them, some standing up and some struggling along the ground; instead of a smooth

CENTRAL PARK'S MUSEUMS

Although, as Central Park historian Sara Cedar Miller observes, "Olmsted and Vaux did not promote Central Park as a civic center featuring cultural, artistic, and scientific institutions," in their Greensward Plan the two designers suggested that a small museum be placed in the arsenal in the park's southeastern corner. Built in 1851, the arsenal originally served as a munitions storage facility for the New York State National Guard before it was converted to offices for the park's administrators in 1857.

Despite Olmsted and Vaux's recommendation, a museum did not open in the arsenal until more than a decade after construction began on Central Park. In 1871, the recently founded American Museum of Natural History set up exhibits of mounted mammals and birds in the former munitions depot. Six years later—having long since outgrown the arsenal—the museum was moved to a new building designed by Vaux and his assistant, Jacob Wrey Mould, on Manhattan Square, across the street from Central Park between West 77th and 81st streets.

The second important museum associated with Central Park is the Metropolitan Museum of Art, or the Met. Incorporated in 1870, by 1872 turf surface of clean short grass there should be varied sorts of herbage one crowding over another and all running together without any order, or there should be vines and creepers and mosses and ferns."

In addition to using plantings to screen out the distractions of the city and enhance the beauty of the park's various landscapes, Olmsted wanted to make Central Park "an international arboretum of such distinction as to startle the world," notes Eugene Kinkead in his history of Central Park. (An arboretum is a tract of land on which trees and other woody plants are grown for display or study.) By the late 1860s, Olmsted and Pilat had

the Metropolitan Museum of Art had already outgrown two downtown buildings when the state legislature authorized the Department of Parks to raise a half million dollars for the construction of a new museum within Central Park. Designed by Vaux and Mould, the red brick Gothic Revival–style building officially opened in 1880 on the park's eastern edge, facing Fifth Avenue near 81st Street. Gothic Revival—a popular style of architecture in North America and Europe during much of the nineteenth century—imitated many of the elements of medieval European architecture, including steeply pitched roofs, pointed-arch windows, and towers and turrets.

In 1888, the Met was significantly enlarged, and six years later the prominent New York architect Richard M. Hunt drew up plans for a new building that would surround Vaux and Mould's original brick structure on all sides. During the course of the next century, the museum gained additional floors and wings, eventually expanding to cover 14 acres of parkland and become the largest art museum in the Western Hemisphere.

introduced well over 300 species of trees to the park grounds, the vast majority of them nonnatives, including the Siberian Crab, the European Nettle, and the Chinese Elm.

Olmsted's penchant for exotic plants caused him to make a major blunder soon after the park opened. Inspired by a recent trip he had taken to Panama, he directed Pilat to transform the 30-acre wooded Ramble into an imitation Central American jungle by training luxuriant vines—including the highly invasive wisteria—up many of its taller trees. What Olmsted did not realize was that, if left unchecked, the constricting wisteria vine eventually strangles its host tree. After the host tree dies and falls, the fast-growing vine then spreads along the ground until it finds another tree to ascend, and the whole process begins all over again. A number of the park's trees were lost in this way during the decades after the wisteria vine was introduced, and today wisteria has a prominent place on Central Park's official "Do Not Plant" list.

FINANCIAL WORRIES AND A POWER STRUGGLE

Under Olmsted, Waring, and Grant's adept supervision, by 1860 most of the lower park had been reshaped to create the gently rolling meadows, elegant pedestrian mall, and sunken transverse roads called for in the Greensward Plan. Aside from the outstanding managerial skills of the architect in chief and his two top engineers, the main reason that the work on the lower park progressed as rapidly as it did from 1858 to 1860 was the sharp increase in the number of park laborers employed by the city during this period. In April 1858, Olmsted had approximately a thousand men on the job; by October, that number had more than doubled. At the peak of construction in the autumn of 1859, as many as 3,600 men—mainly unskilled laborers but also blacksmiths, stonemasons, carpenters, and gardeners—could be found working in the park on any given day.

While the park's large workforce was busy dredging, grading, planting, and paving, visitors were already beginning to pour into New York's vast new public space. Ice-skating on the lake was a popular pastime in the winter months; during the warmer months, the park's new bridle paths and paved drives attracted upper-class horseback riders and carriage owners. Beginning in 1859, the board began to sponsor free Saturday afternoon band concerts, which typically attracted huge crowds. That summer, Olmsted estimated that as many as 100,000 visitors could be found in the park on most weekend afternoons.

Given the popularity of the infant park, "Olmsted should have been basking in the satisfaction of a job well done," notes Witold Rybczynski in *A Clearing in the Distance: Frederick Law Olmsted and America in the Nineteenth Century*. Instead he found himself increasingly under fire from the park commissioners to slash construction costs. The board had cause for concern: The state legislature had originally authorized $1.5 million in 1857 for the construction of Central Park. By early 1860, it was evident that at least three times that amount would be needed to complete the park according to Olmsted and Vaux's ambitious landscaping scheme. Under pressure from the legislators in Albany, the commissioners postponed some of the work that was supposed to be done on the park's northern portion. Plans to construct an extensive flower garden and a music hall near the mall—both required elements in the design contest of 1857–1858—were shelved for good.

Far more distressing to Olmsted than the loss of the formal garden and the music hall, neither of which had been compatible with the Greensward Plan's bucolic vision in the first place, was the loss of independence he suffered as a result of the park's budgetary issues. In October 1859, the park board appointed one of their own, Commissioner Andrew Haswell Green, to serve as Central Park's comptroller. Authoritarian and extremely budget conscious, Green compelled the architect in chief to obtain his

BUILDING AMERICA NOW

SEATTLE'S FREEWAY PARK

The most striking feature of Seattle, Washington's Freeway Park is that it spans a major transport route—the Interstate 5 freeway—as the highway passes just east of downtown. When it first opened in the early 1970s, Freeway Park had the distinction of being the first American park ever to be built over a freeway. Since then, several other U.S. cities have either built or developed plans to build highway parks. Among the most notable of these are Phoenix's 10-acre Margaret T. Hance Park atop Interstate 10 and the Rose Kennedy Greenway atop Boston's "Big Dig," a mammoth construction project that rerouted several miles of Interstate 93 into a tunnel that runs underneath the city.

Financed by federal and city funds, Freeway Park cost just over $4 million to construct. This 5.2-acre urban oasis, designed by landscape architect Lawrence Halprin and his associate Angela Danadjieva, features a variety of trees and shrubs; a series of angular, interlocking concrete walls and planting containers that divide the park into a number of different outdoor "rooms"; and a central waterfall that plunges dramatically over a 30-foot-tall concrete canyon. The thunderous noise of the waterfall cascading into the canyon helps muffle the incessant drone of the Interstate 5 traffic below.

Freeway Park was a popular destination for Seattle residents and tourists when it first opened in the early 1970s. Visitor numbers declined sharply during the 1990s and early 2000s, however, after drug sellers and users began to frequent the park and several widely publicized murders and rapes took place there. Recently, efforts have been made to revitalize the park by making it safer. More pedestrian lighting and directional signs have been installed, and trees have been removed or pruned in certain areas to create open spaces and increase visibility.

prior approval for every expenditure, no matter how trivial. Green's stranglehold over the budget made Olmsted furious; he believed that the penny-pinching Green was usurping his rightful authority and hampering his and Vaux's ability to realize their design plan for the park. "Not a dollar, not a cent, is got from under [Green's] paw that is not wet with his blood & sweat," Olmsted wrote angrily to a friend in early 1861. When the Civil War broke out that April, Olmsted's bitter power struggle with Green came to an abrupt end. Shortly after the war began, Olmsted—a firm supporter of the Union cause—left New York for Washington, D.C., for a time to assume the position of executive secretary of the U.S. Sanitary Commission, the precursor of the American Red Cross.

LANDSCAPING THE UPPER PARK

Following Olmsted's departure for Washington in 1861, the building of the park advanced at a slower pace. With the lower park all but complete, the focus now moved to the northern half of the park, above the old rectangular municipal reservoir, or the lower reservoir, as it was generally known. Much of the area already comprised gently rolling plains, so creating the vast stretches of meadowland that the Greensward Plan called for was not as expensive and labor intensive in the upper park as it had been in the park's southern portion.

In 1863, the northern boundaries of Central Park were extended northward from 106th Street to 110th Street, adding 65 acres to the park, which now encompassed a total of 843 acres. The Board of Commissioners had been able to obtain the additional land at a very low price because it was deemed too swampy and rocky for real estate development. The board had first committed itself to acquiring the land north of 106th Street in 1859, so Olmsted and Vaux had developed a design plan for the new addition several years before the tract was actually purchased. They proposed to leave the ruggedly picturesque areas as natural as possible, a scheme that had obvious appeal for

The last section of the park to be completed included Harlem Meer *(above)*, the second-largest body of water in Central Park. Renovated in the 1990s, the meer has become one of the most beautiful locations in the park, but it is still faithful to Olmsted and Vaux's original plan for the area.

the money-conscious board and the frugal comptroller Green. Olmsted and Vaux did, however, direct that a big manmade lake be excavated in the lowest-lying section of the park's brand-new northeastern corner. The 11-acre body of water was dubbed the Harlem Meer because its site was once a part of the Dutch American village of Harlem. Dramatic natural rock outcroppings and a large ravine—which the two designers had planted with a wide variety of native and nonnative trees, including bald cypress, oak, beech, and ginkgo—bordered the meer. A 14-foot-tall artificial waterfall would also eventually be constructed in the wooded landscape surrounding the meer and, to the lake's west, the highest peak in a chain of schist outcroppings would be fashioned into the meadow-topped Great Hill. On the Great Hill's summit, park visitors could enjoy a panoramic view of the Hudson River and the Palisades, the steep cliffs that border the Hudson's western bank.

While Olmsted and Vaux were working out a plan for the new parkland north of 106th Street, Vaux was also beginning to plot designs for the park's numerous architectural structures. The graceful and unique structures that Calvert Vaux fashioned for Central Park during the 1860s, which included dozens of simple yet elegant bridges and arched passageways—as well as his masterpiece, stately Bethesda Terrace—would make up one of the most ambitious and celebrated architectural programs ever created for a public park.

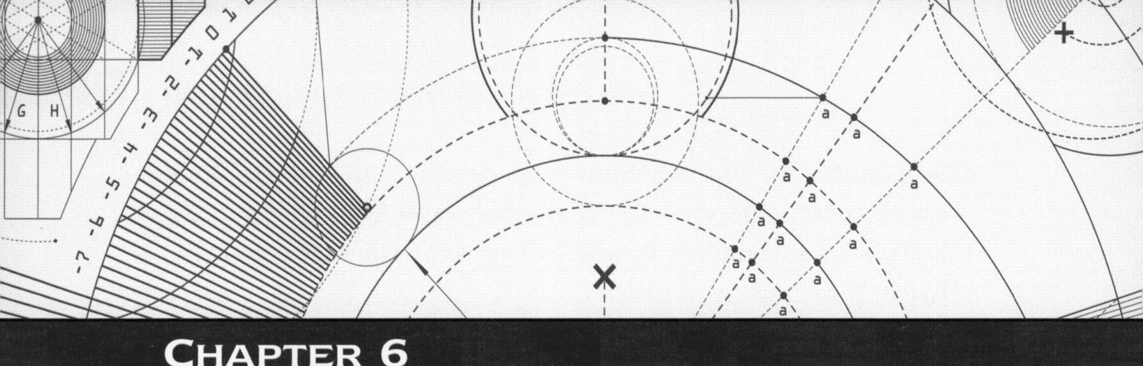

CHAPTER 6

Central Park's Unique Architecture

Focused as it was on creating a simple, rural refuge in the heart of the city, Frederick Law Olmsted and Calvert Vaux's design plan for Central Park paid little attention to architectural structures, with the exception of calling for a formal terrace that would overlook the large lake in the park's midsection. The separate internal circulation systems that Olmsted and Vaux decided to create for carriage, pedestrian, and horseback traffic shortly after the Board of Commissioners selected the Greensward Plan, however, required the building of numerous bridges and underpasses wherever the park's 70 miles of bridle paths, drives, and walkways intersected. During the first decade after the park opened, Olmsted and Vaux also approved the construction of dozens of overlooks, shelters, boathouses, and other architectural structures, designed both for the convenience of park users and to enhance the beauty of the park's landscapes.

Because of his formal training in architecture, Vaux took chief responsibility for designing Central Park's early structures.

Assisting him on many of these building projects was Jacob Wrey Mould, another English-born architect. Mould's specialty was architectural ornamentalism—adding decorative elements to a building or other structure to enhance its appearance—and he was known for his ability to work equally well with a variety of materials, including stone, metal, and brick.

BETHESDA TERRACE

Stately Bethesda Terrace—conceived by Olmsted and Vaux as a place to socialize as well as to contemplate nature—is Central Park's most impressive architectural space. "At the Terrace," writes Sara Cedar Miller in *Central Park, an American Masterpiece*, "Vaux merged the naturalistic landscape with an ambitious architectural program, the vision and scope of which was never again matched in any other public park." Vaux himself was prouder of the terrace than of any other architectural structure he designed for Central Park. The ultimate success of the terrace design, Vaux believed, rested on his command of "light and shade and play of line . . . the weaving of the Landscape into the Architecture and the Architecture into the Landscape." As Vaux observed to a reporter while the terrace was still under construction, his first principle in park design was "Nature first, second and third—Architecture after a while."

The terrace was begun in 1859, not long after the completion of the butterfly-shaped lake it bordered, and it was largely finished by 1865. It was constructed from imported Canadian sandstone because Vaux thought that its grayish color contrasted nicely with the bright green of the surrounding foliage. Vaux divided the spacious sandstone terrace into three main sections: the upper terrace, the lower terrace, and the arcade, a covered passageway.

The arcade, which runs beneath the Terrace Bridge and the carriage drive, leads pedestrians from the northern end of the mall to the waterside lower terrace. To reach the 29-foot-wide and

16-foot-high arcade from the mall, Vaux had visitors descend a broad stairway flanked on either side by tall sandstone end posts or piers. The piers were decorated with ornate and imaginative panels designed by Jacob Mould and created in place by skilled stone carvers. The panels' "day" carvings, which were meant to symbolize the times of the day, included detailed depictions of a crowing rooster and a rising sun; the "night" carvings included whimsical renditions of an owl, a bat, and the familiar Halloween symbols of a jack-o'-lantern and a witch on a broomstick.

According to Vaux's design, the chief visual element of the long, columned arcade was its massive ceiling, which he and

Of the seven ornamental fountains in Central Park, Bethesda Fountain *(above)* is the most famous and popular of them all. Constructed near a large, intricately designed stone terrace, Bethesda Fountain features the sculpture *Angel of Waters*, which has become one of the most recognizable icons of the park. Beautiful and serene, the fountain is frequently used as a filming location for television and movies.

Mould had covered with nearly 16,000 handcrafted ceramic tiles. Designed by Mould and produced by the Minton Company of Stoke-on-Trent, England, the one-inch-thick tiles were encaustic, which meant that their patterns were made by inlaying different colored clays into the body of the tile rather than by the usual method of applying a surface glaze. Vaux and Mould used mechanical fasteners to attach the jewel-like tiles, which together weighed 50 tons, to a gilded wrought-iron frame suspended from the arcade's ceiling. The brilliantly hued tiles were arranged in an arabesque design, a type of ornate decoration associated with Islamic art that typically features leaves, branches, flowers, and geometric figures intertwined in a complex pattern.

Vaux and Mould clearly viewed the arcade's exotic and colorful ceiling as the focal point of the underground pedestrian passageway. To serve as the upper terrace's visual center of interest they designed two monumental and lavishly decorated stone stairways, which flank the space on either side and descend to the terrace's spacious lower section. Mould, who appropriately chose nature as his theme, adorned the cascading staircases' balustrades (railings) and piers with intricate and remarkably accurate carvings of animals, birds, and plants to symbolize the four seasons. "Sensuous details such as the grapes and tendrils below the stag on the autumn pier or a group of brilliantly tactile [touchable] and playful icicles . . . on the western side of the winter pier—display a breathtaking sensitivity on the part of both Mould and the excellent carvers who brought his two-dimensional drawings to life," writes one of Mould's most enthusiastic modern admirers, author Sara Cedar Miller.

ANGEL OF THE WATERS

To serve as the visual centerpiece of the third and final section of the terrace, the lower terrace, Vaux designed an imposing yet simple fountain that featured a 96-foot-diameter circular stone basin capable of holding 52,000 gallons of water. Even before construction began on the terrace, the park board selected artist Emma Stebbins to create a bronze sculpture to adorn the simple water jet, which made Stebbins the first woman to receive a major public commission in New York City. Modeled in Rome, where Stebbins maintained a studio, and cast in Munich, Germany, the *Angel of the Waters* ultimately cost $63,000, a sum that some critics attacked as exorbitant, even though the statue was largely paid for by private donations rather than public funds. Others derided the 8-foot-tall sculpture as unattractive

VAUX AND MOULD'S EXOTIC MINERAL SPRINGS PAVILION

The exotic Mineral Springs Pavilion, designed by Calvert Vaux and Jacob Wrey Mould, was constructed on the park's southwestern side—near Eighth Avenue and 70th Street—in the late 1860s. Once one of Central Park's most distinctive and popular architectural structures, during the 1960s the aging brick pavilion was demolished and replaced by a small cafe.

Old photographs reveal that the Mineral Spring Pavilion's fanciful, Moorish-inspired design included a dramatic flaring roof and pointed arches supported on slender columns. Decorated with colorful tile and stenciling, the pavilion's ornate and luxurious interior featured a large marble hexagonal counter where park visitors could order glasses of mineral water dispensed from elegant silver faucets. Many leading nineteenth-century physicians and health reformers were firm believers in the benefits of drinking mineral water, which they recommended as a cure for a wide array of illnesses and medical conditions as well as for alcoholism. The mineral water that flowed from the Mineral Spring Pavilion's posh faucets was not authentic, however; it was city water that had been doctored to taste like water from the world's best-known natural springs.

and ungainly; it looked, one writer snobbishly complained, like a "servant girl executing a polka." Most of the criticism of *Angel of the Waters*, however, centered on the board's choice of Stebbins for the project; the sculptress just happened to be the sister of park board president Henry G. Stebbins.

Despite the press's widespread charges of nepotism (showing favoritism on the basis of family relationship by those in power), Stebbins's sculpture of a winged female figure blessing the water beneath her was an immediate hit with the public and quickly became one of Central Park's most beloved icons. At the dedication ceremony in May 1873, Stebbins revealed that she associated the terrace fountain with the healing Pool of Bethesda described in the Bible. From that point forward, the fountain was known as Bethesda Fountain, and the terrace—which Vaux and Olmsted had referred to simply as the "Water Terrace" in their Greensward Plan—became known as the Bethesda Terrace.

BELVEDERE CASTLE

Following the end of the Civil War in 1865, Calvert Vaux—with the approval of his Greensward partner, Frederick Law Olmsted—designed a number of unique and fanciful architectural structures for Central Park, including numerous shelters, boathouses, and lookouts. The best known of these various structures is Belvedere Castle, which Vaux had constructed astride Vista Rock in 1867. *Belvedere*, an Italian word that means "beautiful view," is in architectural terms a structure designed to look out on a pleasing vista, and Vaux's imitation medieval fortress more than lived up to its name. Resting atop the second highest point in Central Park, Belvedere Castle was well situated to afford visitors panoramic views of both the park and the city.

Yet Vaux did not intend Belvedere Castle to serve only as an observation tower. He also wanted the exotic structure to be a focal point for park visitors who looked out across the lake from the mall or the terrace, drawing their gaze to what he and Olmsted considered the park's chief natural feature: craggy Vista

Calvert Vaux wanted to design a fanciful structure that would attract visitors to Vista Rock. Drawing on medieval influences, Vaux built Belvedere Castle *(above)* on the second-highest point of the park, allowing visitors to see a panoramic view of the area.

Rock. In this sense, Belvedere Castle followed in the tradition of a folly, a whimsical form of architecture that was especially popular in eighteenth-century England. Follies were fanciful structures, such as miniaturized castles or fake Roman ruins, meant to attract attention to an interesting vista or evoke the romantic taste of another time or place.

In keeping with Vaux's maxim, "Nature First, Second, and Third—Architecture after a while," Belvedere Castle was designed to blend seamlessly with the building's rugged site; most of the ersatz fortress was fashioned from the same hard, ash gray schist as Vista Rock itself. Inside the building, Vaux placed a narrow staircase leading up to lookouts from the upper terrace and turret. Although the castle has been enclosed since 1919, when the U.S. Weather Bureau set up a lab there, it was actually built as a shell with no windows or doors. Vaux's initial design for Belvedere Castle included a second two-story schist structure with a corner turret to the west of the main structure, but—owing to financial concerns—a more modest open wood pavilion was constructed in its place in 1871.

CENTRAL PARK'S ARCHES AND BRIDGES

For many of Central Park's admirers, its most defining architectural feature is its many charming bridges and arches, no two of which are alike. Most of these simple yet elegant structures were the creations of Calvert Vaux. Between 1859 and 1875, the English-born architect oversaw the construction of 35 unique bridges and arched passageways throughout the park. Only a few of the structures actually spanned water: The majority were designed to ensure the safety of visitors who used different modes of transportation by separating pedestrian, carriage, and horseback traffic wherever the park's bridle trails, carriage drives, and footways intersected. Relying on a variety of natural and man-made substances, including stone, wood, brick, and cast iron, Vaux endeavored to achieve harmony in material and design between each of the nearly three dozen different bridges and arches he designed for Central Park and their specific landscapes. "For the most part," wrote the author and journalist Clarence Cook in 1873, New York's "bridges are as ugly as engineers, with their dry-as-dust brains can devise." Yet in Central Park, he noted admiringly, "the effort was made to have the bridges not only solidly built, but as elegantly and in as great variety of designs, as could be contrived."

Unquestionably, the best known of Vaux's Central Park bridges are three of the five cast-iron bridges he designed for the park: Bow Bridge, which spans about 60 feet of the lake; Pine Bank Bridge, which traverses the southern end of the bridle trail;

and Gothic Bridge, which crosses the bridle trail on the northern side of the large, irregularly shaped municipal reservoir today known as the Jacqueline Kennedy Onassis Reservoir. Because cast iron was strong, readily available, and inexpensive, it was a favorite building material during the mid- to late nineteenth century. Between 1839, when America's first entirely iron bridge was erected in Brownsville, Pennsylvania, and about 1880, when it was superceded by lighter, stronger steel, cast iron was used to construct several thousand bridges throughout the United States.

Completed in 1862, light and graceful Bow Bridge is one of the most photographed bridges in the world. The bridge's name derives from its distinctive shape, which is curved like an archer's bow. To create Bow Bridge and the park's other cast-iron bridges, Vaux and Mould drew the structures' various parts in meticulous detail, then sent their plans to the iron foundry for casting. Bow Bridge's stunning iron railing combines elements of classical Greek, Renaissance, and Gothic Revival design and features intricate foliate (leaf-like) designs and cinquefoils (ornamental carvings that consist of five intersecting arcs arranged in a circle). Pine Bank Bridge, which is nestled scenically between two large schist outcroppings and was completed several months before Bow Bridge, boasts intricate latticework on its gently curved cast-iron railing. Built in 1864, Gothic Bridge, the last of the great iron bridges created by Vaux and Mould, was named for the distinctive style of its spandrels, the roughly triangular shape between the curve of an arch and its surround. To make the large spandrels on either side of the bridge, Vaux and Mould used gracefully curved ironwork in a lace cutout design reminiscent of the Gothic Church architecture of medieval Europe.

Fashioned from brick and a variety of stones and often equipped with seats and drinking fountains, the numerous arches that Vaux created for Central Park conveyed pedestrians and horseback riders safely beneath the park's busy carriage drives. Yet, Vaux's arches were not only highly functional; each one was also a work of art, with some designed in a stately, ornate style and others in a naturalistic, rustic style.

One of the most richly decorated of Vaux's Central Park arches is striking Greywacke Arch, located near the Metropolitan Museum. Fashioned from brownstone and greywacke—a type of gray sandstone—arranged in alternating patterns, Greywacke Arch features exotic, spade-shaped archways with Middle Eastern overtones. Standing in sharp contrast to the ornate elegance and carefully ordered patterns of Greywacke are the rough-hewn styles of two of Vaux's most picturesque rustic arches, Glen Span and Huddlestone. Both arches carry sections of the West Drive in the park's northern section and serve as gateways into the wooded ravine—Glen Span from the west and Huddlestone from the northeast. Vaux sought to give Glen Span Arch a naturalistic, untamed quality by piling up uncut schist boulders at the base of the arch's simple stone abutments (the parts of a structure that support the weight or pressure of an arch). For the cave-like Huddlestone Arch, Vaux used massive schist boulders from around the park, one of which reputedly weighed more than 100 tons, to fashion the entire structure. Remarkably, no mortar or metal supports were used in the construction of the 10-foot-high, 22-foot-wide Huddlestone Arch; gravity and friction alone keep it standing.

THE CHILDREN'S DISTRICT AND TAMMANY HALL

During the early years of Central Park's existence, Olmsted and Vaux were chastised by the New York press for all but ignoring the park's youngest visitors in their Greensward Plan. In response to this criticism, the Board of Commissioners directed the two designers to set aside a portion of the lower park for the use of children and their caregivers. The area that Olmsted chose for the Children's District, as he dubbed it, was located just south of the 65th Street transverse road and north of the pond. During New York's hot, muggy summers, notes author Eugene Kinkead, the Children's District "was cooled by a southerly breeze drawn off the Pond." According to Kinkead, Olmsted had long been appalled by the crowded, unhealthy conditions in which many of the city's working-class children lived. When Olmsted formulated his plans for the Children's District, he decided that keeping poor youngsters and their mothers cool in the dog days of summer "was just the kind of service he wanted the Park to render," asserts Kinkead: "Infant and child mortality in the city increased sharply in the dog days, and families that could not leave town

BUILDING AMERICA NOW

MILLENNIUM PARK'S AMAZING MUSIC PAVILION

Among the many distinctive architectural structures created for Chicago's Millennium Park are the Frank Gehry–designed BP Bridge, a serpentine, steel-sheathed pedestrian bridge that connects the park to Daley Bicentennial Plaza; and the McDonald's Cycle Center, a solar-heated, indoor bicycle parking facility where bicycle commuters can lock up their bikes, shower, and buy breakfast before heading off to work in downtown Chicago. Yet unquestionably, the architectural showcase of Chicago's grand new public space is the Jay Pritzker Pavilion, Frank Gehry's immense, shimmering band shell. Crowned by a gigantic headdress of billowing stainless-steel ribbons, the 120-foot-high music pavilion is the visual centerpiece of the entire park.

Building Gehry's elaborately designed structure was an extremely complex, time-consuming, and expensive process; the pavilion's final price tag came to just over $60 million, nearly six times its original budget. Construction on the band shell began in early 2002, and by the end of the year the pavilion's concrete superstructure was suffered most. For them, Olmsted said, 'the best that can be done is to spend an occasional day or part of the day in the Park.'"

Vaux, with Olmsted's blessing, created two main structures for the Children's District: the dairy, to dispense fresh milk and other refreshments, and the Kinderberg Shelter (Kinderberg is German for "children's mountain"), which stood across from the dairy on the crest of a small rock outcropping. The stone dairy, which was designed in Gothic Revival style, featured church-like spires and window treatments, vivid orange trim, and an

completed. Workers next began working on the band shell's soaring, curved headdress, using a triple-girder crane to transport its 679 interlocking stainless-steel panels. The gigantic crane was so heavy that it arrived on the construction site in pieces to avoid cracking the roadway below. By late 2003, the flamboyant headdress, which extends from 90 to 100 feet above the band shell's large, wood-lined stage, had finally been attached.

In July 2004, two years after work began on Gehry's dramatic outdoor concert venue, the Jay Pritzker Pavilion was officially opened to enormous acclaim. Critics and the general public alike were impressed not only by the pavilion's stunning appearance but also by its state-of-the-art trellised sound system. The gigantic overhead sound system—a completely welded steel structure—connects to the band shell's huge steel mane and extends across the entire width of the Great Lawn, a 600-acre green in front of the pavilion that can accommodate an audience of 12,000. Composed of crisscrossing, curved steel pipes with diameters of just 15 inches, the trellis is a remarkably light structure that gracefully frames the Chicago skyline while providing concertgoers with a sound system that rivals those of the world's top indoor music venues.

ornate wooden loggia (roofed porch) with open sides to catch the refreshing breezes that wafted in off the pond. Just to the west of the dairy, the octagonal Kinderberg Shelter, constructed entirely from the rough, unmilled branches of cedar trees and featuring a diameter of over 100 feet, was far and away the largest rustic shelter in the park. By the 1930s, however, the massive structure was in need of extensive repair. Unfortunately, instead of trying to salvage the whimsical shelter, park administrators decided to tear it down. Since 1952, a small red and white brick building known as the Chess and Checkers House has stood on the site of Vaux's rustic masterpiece.

In 1870, as construction on the dairy and the Kinderberg Shelter neared completion, the powerful and corrupt Manhattan political boss William Marcy Tweed and his Tammany Hall cronies (named for Tweed's New York headquarters) gained control of the city council and the park board. In direct opposition to Olmsted and Vaux's wishes, Central Park's new administrators immediately transformed the dairy from a healthful retreat for children into a restaurant for all park users. The board—eager to create new jobs for their working-class supporters while also catering to the wishes of many middle- and upper-class New Yorkers—initiated other park "improvement" projects against the designers' objections. Most significantly, they had Olmsted and Vaux's gracefully curving carriage drives straightened to allow carriages to move more quickly through the park, and dozens of trees along the park's perimeter were cut down or severely pruned to provide adjacent homeowners with an unhindered view of its lush meadows and gardens.

In late 1877, the park's Tammany Hall administrators, fed up with Olmsted's outspoken criticism of their pet projects, informed him that his nearly 20-year tenure with Central Park was finished. Although his many admirers in New York were outraged by the board's decision, Olmsted made no effort to contest his dismissal: The park's construction was now essentially

Olmsted and Vaux created a complex network of pedestrian, carriage, bicycle, and bridle paths inside the park. Vaux designed all the bridges in Central Park to allow different paths to cross without disrupting the pace or environment of visitors. *Above*, a pedestrian bridge rises above a horse path.

finished, and he was anxious to focus on other landscaping projects. During the next several decades, Olmsted helped design dozens of acclaimed public and private green spaces in cities and towns across the United States and Canada, including Montreal's Mount Royal Park; the Biltmore Estate in Asheville, North Carolina; and Boston's famous Emerald Necklace, a verdant, six-mile stretch of parks and parkways. Vaux, who worked with Olmsted on several major landscaping projects during the 1860s and early

1870s—including Brooklyn's Prospect Park—continued to work intermittently on architectural assignments for Central Park until his death from drowning in 1895.

Olmsted and Vaux's rural refuge in the heart of Manhattan, which was under construction for nearly two decades, had required the efforts of thousands of skilled and unskilled laborers and some $14 million (more than $250 million today) to complete. Yet the authors of the Greensward Plan never doubted for a moment that New York City's first great public park was worth such a massive investment of money and manpower. "The time will come when New York will be built up," Olmsted predicted in 1858,

> when all the grading and filling will be done, and when the picturesquely-varied, rocky formations of the Island will have been converted into foundations for rows of monotonous straight streets, and piles of erect, angular buildings. There will be no suggestion left of its present varied surface, with the single exception of the Park. Then the priceless value of . . . [its] picturesque outlines . . . will be more distinctively perceived.

CHAPTER 7

A Work in Progress: Central Park Since 1877

During the more than a century and a quarter since 1877, the year the park is generally considered to have been completed according to Frederick Law Olmsted and Calvert Vaux's Greensward Plan, Central Park has remained very much a work in progress. New buildings and attractions have been added, original structures have been torn down or rebuilt, and various modifications have been made to the park's landscape and infrastructure.

HECKSCHER PLAYGROUND AND THE LOWER RESERVOIR

With two notable exceptions, little changed in Central Park during the first five decades after Olmsted's professional association with the park ended in 1877. In 1912, the park's gravel carriage drives were covered in asphalt to make them more suitable for its increasing automobile traffic. Then, nearly a decade and a half later in 1926, Central Park finally got its first equipped playground.

Although equipped playgrounds in parks and other public spaces were common in New York and many other American cities by the 1920s, the creation of Central Park's first modern play space for children in 1926 was a source of considerable controversy. The trouble began when New York financier and real estate magnate August Heckscher Sr. offered a state-of-the-art playground to the park, complete with swings, slides, jungle gyms, seesaws, merry-go-rounds, a spacious field house,

BUILDING AMERICA NOW

MILLENNIUM PARK'S MONUMENTAL ARTWORK

Although Olmsted and Vaux urged that bronze statues of prominent Americans be placed in Central Park's most formal space—the terrace—they hoped to otherwise keep large pieces of sculpture in Central Park to a minimum, viewing them as an unnecessary distraction from their serene rural landscape. Nonetheless, by 1900 the park boasted 24 statues, and by 2000, there were more than 50. Most were donated by individuals or organizations, including different ethnic organizations eager to commemorate their homeland's cultural and political heroes, such as German composer Ludwig van Beethoven and Italian revolutionary and patriot Giuseppe Mazzini.

In stark contrast to Olmsted and Vaux's negative attitude toward placing large pieces of sculpture in Central Park, from the very beginning the creators of Millennium Park envisioned Chicago's new public space as an outdoor art museum as well as a landscaped park. Accordingly, they chose two of the most influential sculptors of the late twentieth and early twenty-first centuries, Anish Kapoor of the United Kingdom and Jaume Plensa of Spain, to create massive pieces of public art for the new project.

and a wading pool. Heckscher soon discovered that convincing the park board to accept his generous gift would be no easy matter.

At the heart of the board members' reluctance to install the playground was their fear of angering Central Park's well-to-do neighbors. A number of them strongly objected to the proposed play space on the grounds that it would attract droves of noisy, working-class children and their families to the park.

At 66 feet long, 42 feet wide, and 33 feet high, Kapoor's *Cloud Gate* is one of the largest outdoor sculptures in the world. The bean-shaped sculpture, constructed at a cost of more than $20 million, is composed of 168 stainless-steel plates fastened to internal scaffolding. Designed to resemble liquid mercury, its curved, highly polished surface reflects clouds, skyscrapers that surround the park on two sides, and pedestrians passing by. The sculpture's interactive qualities have made it one of the park's—and the city's—most famous and popular attractions.

Jaume Plensa's massive *Crown Fountain* also quickly become one of Chicago's best-known and loved works of public art after Millennium Park opened in 2004. It consists of two 50-foot glass brick towers that face each other across a shallow, 4-foot-wide pool paved in black granite. Behind the transparent glass bricks are more than a million state-of-the-art light-emitting diodes (LEDs), which turn the towers into giant video screens. Each screen scrolls through videos of a thousand ordinary Chicagoans. At timed intervals, the faces on the two towers purse their lips and water flows out—a sort of high-tech, twenty-first-century version of the water-spouting stone gargoyles that often decorated fountains in Renaissance Europe.

Heckscher, however, was persistent. The German immigrant and self-made millionaire was an enthusiastic supporter of the so-called "playground movement" of the late nineteenth and early twentieth centuries, which stressed the importance of providing underprivileged urban children with opportunities for safe outdoor recreation. Heckscher had already funded the construction of several equipped playgrounds in Lower Manhattan and viewed the Central Park project as a personal crusade. When the wealthy philanthropist finally persuaded park officials to stand up to the park's snobbish neighbors and accept the play equipment, the nearly 4-acre Heckscher Playground became the first part of Central Park to be privately funded. Constructed in the southwestern portion of the park at 61st Street and Seventh Avenue, it quickly became one of Central Park's most heavily used amenities.

Aside from the controversy over placing an equipped playground in the park, the other major area of contention regarding Central Park in the 1920s centered on the lower reservoir, the older and more southerly of the two municipal receiving pools located between 79th and 96th streets. By 1920, the New York Water Department was no longer using the 35-acre lower reservoir, and plans were being drawn up to drain it. The question of what to do with the new parkland that would be created once the reservoir was emptied was endlessly debated in City Hall and the local press. A number of very different ideas were put forth, including converting the land into an airfield, a sports complex, a memorial to fallen World War I soldiers, or a mammoth underground parking lot. Finally, in 1930, park officials decided to adopt the American Society of Landscape Architects' (ASLA) recommendation to turn the site into a large, oval-shaped meadow. Of all the various proposals, the board concluded, only the ASLA's suggestion was in keeping with Olmsted and Vaux's original vision of the park as a rural retreat in the heart of Manhattan.

Heckscher Playground *(above)* is the largest children's play area in Central Park. With water features, seesaws, swings, a wooden suspension bridge, and nearby ball fields, Heckscher Playground rose above the controversy over its creation to become one of the most popular children's spots in the park.

In 1931, after a decade of wrangling about the future of the lower reservoir site, the obsolete receiving pool was finally drained. Yet, with New York mired in the Great Depression, the severe economic downturn that plagued the United States during the 1930s, city officials put off the expensive task of filling the 35-acre reservoir and converting it into meadowland. Consequently, the site served as a makeshift home for some of the hundreds of thousands of New Yorkers who were thrown out of work by the Depression. Until they were finally evicted in 1933, dozens

REBUILDING CENTRAL PARK: A MANAGEMENT AND RESTORATION PLAN

In 1985, Elizabeth Barlow Rogers and the Central Park Conservancy published a detailed proposal for the rebuilding and management of Central Park entitled *Rebuilding Central Park: A Management and Restoration Plan*. In the publication, Rogers noted that the condition of New York City's premier public space at the time of the conservancy's founding five years earlier "was truly shocking." According to *Rebuilding Central Park*, six guiding principles have been at the heart of the conservancy's ambitious restoration and management plan for the park:

- ★ Protection and preservation—It is imperative that its custodians do not accept invasion by other interests and that no further portions of it be dedicated to a single interest group.
- ★ Historic character—It does not require a period restoration correct to the last detail but rather the use of the Greensward Plan, wherever possible, as reference and guide.
- ★ Public safety and enjoyment—It is not enough that a park be safe; it must appear to be safe as well. Vandalized structures and park furniture create an atmosphere of lawlessness and gloom.
- ★ Maintaining cleanliness and structural soundness—Good routine maintenance and consistent public education build respect for the park.
- ★ Horticultural beauty and ecological health—Good forestry and horticultural practices are essential to ensure the park's continued beauty and health, and are made more urgent because of the heavy volume of use of Central Park.
- ★ Functional and structural integrity—Fragmented administration of design maintenance and operations needs to be overcome.

of destitute squatters made their homes in ramshackle huts on the old reservoir bed, which was variously referred to in the New York press as "Shanty Village," "Shack Town," and "Forgotten Man's Gulch."

COMMISSIONER ROBERT MOSES PUTS HIS STAMP ON CENTRAL PARK

In 1934, Robert Moses became the first New York parks commissioner to oversee a citywide Department of Parks, which covered the five boroughs (administrative divisions) of the Bronx, Brooklyn, Queens, Staten Island, and Manhattan. Upon assuming office, the energetic and efficient Moses immediately started work on Central Park's vast new mid-park meadow, dubbed the Great Lawn. Moses took advantage of federal relief programs, using government money to hire the small army of laborers required to fill in the cavernous reservoir and fashion the oval Great Lawn, which today remains the single largest design feature in Central Park that was not included in Olmsted and Vaux's Greensward Plan.

By the end of the 1930s, Moses had also tapped federal relief funds to open a new restaurant (the celebrated Tavern on the Green), construct more than 20 fully equipped playgrounds and numerous athletic fields, repair pathways and roads, reseed meadows, and plant or prune trees and shrubs throughout Central Park. Moses's most famous and widely lauded project in Central Park during the Depression, however, was his renovation of the park's zoo. From Central Park's earliest days, a small menagerie composed chiefly of donated animals, ranging from deer and geese to a boa constrictor, had existed in the park's southeastern corner, behind the arsenal. Soon after taking office, Moses launched a major remodeling of the rundown menagerie; its flimsy wire and wooden buildings were demolished, and modern brick and concrete structures were erected in their place, including a spacious outdoor sea lion pool. The new zoo quickly became one of the park's most visited and beloved attractions. (During the late 1980s, after the Wildlife Conservation Society assumed management of the Central Park Zoo, the zoo underwent a second major renovation in which state-of-the-art habitat exhibits designed to resemble the animals' natural environments replaced Moses's long-outdated structures.)

Renovated during the Great Depression, the Central Park Zoo *(above)* was transformed by New York City parks commissioner Robert Moses from a small, rundown menagerie of donated animals into one of the park's most popular attractions. Currently featuring more than 130 species of animals from polar, rain forest, and temperate regions, the zoo also includes a special children's section and petting zoo.

Robert Moses ultimately served for 26 years as New York's commissioner of parks, finally leaving the post in 1960 to help plan the 1964 New York World's Fair. The numerous changes he instigated in Central Park, including construction of the mammoth 33,000-square-foot Wollman Skating Rink on the pond's northern arm and the transformation of dozens of acres of meadowland into soccer fields and baseball diamonds, have made Moses one of the most controversial figures in the park's history. In direct opposition to Olmsted and Vaux's vision of a spacious green oasis where claustrophobic urbanites could quietly contemplate soothing rural scenery, Moses was chiefly concerned with promoting active recreation in Central Park and the other New York City parks he oversaw. Unquestionably, some of Moses's "improvements" to the park—such as demolishing the rustic Kinderberg Shelter, the elegant Marble Arch near the mall, and several other Vaux-designed structures—did irreparable damage to Olmsted and Vaux's masterwork. Nonetheless, many of the park's most popular features (even though they are clearly at odds with Olmsted and Vaux's original intentions) can be credited directly to Moses, including nearly all of its numerous playgrounds, athletic fields, and formal baseball diamonds; the Wollman Rink; and the significantly upgraded Central Park Zoo.

OVERUSE AND A FISCAL CRISIS TAKE THEIR TOLL ON THE PARK

The decades of the 1960s and 1970s proved to be challenging ones for Central Park. During the mid- to late 1960s, two park commissioners, Thomas Hoving and August Heckscher Jr. (the son of the philanthropist), focused on popularizing Central Park, and under their tenures park use increased dramatically. Breaking with precedents set by previous park officials, Hoving and Heckscher actively promoted a wide range of large public events in the park, ranging from free rock concerts to ethnic festivals

In the 1970s, when New York City nearly went bankrupt, the parks department experienced a shortfall in funding and Central Park became neglected and dirty. Many of the park's famous landmarks were shut down. *Above*, a pond in Central Park is clogged with garbage.

to peace rallies. Many of these heavily attended gatherings took place on the Great Lawn, whose once lush grass was all but trampled out of existence by the milling crowds.

As hard as the big public events of the 1960s were on Central Park's fragile ecosystem, even tougher times lay ahead for New York City's most famous public space. During the 1970s, a major fiscal crisis struck the city, and government funding for park maintenance and renovations plummeted. By the end of the decade, the Great Lawn was a veritable dustbowl, Belvedere

Castle had been vandalized so many times that it had to be boarded up, Bethesda Terrace's stately stairways and piers were covered in graffiti, and beer and soda cans filled the lake and Harlem Meer. Although Central Park had been designated as a National Historic Landmark in 1963 and as a New York City Landmark in 1974, neither of these prestigious honors brought the park the funds that were so desperately needed to rehabilitate Frederick Law Olmsted and Calvert Vaux's nineteenth-century masterpiece.

In 1978 and 1979, New York's financial situation began to show signs of improvement, but lending banks demanded continued fiscal austerity from City Hall. If Central Park's former glory was to be restored, it would have to rely on the generosity of the private sector.

THE CENTRAL PARK CONSERVANCY TO THE RESCUE

Olmsted and Vaux's rural sanctuary in midtown Manhattan gained a new lease on life when the Central Park Conservancy, a private, not-for-profit organization, was founded in 1980 by author and landscape designer Elizabeth Barlow Rogers. The conservancy's primary goal was to renovate the park's historic landscapes and structures following nearly 20 years of overuse and neglect. Reflecting a newfound appreciation for Central Park's value to the city (and the country as a whole) as well as for its fragility, individuals, foundations, and corporations throughout New York and the United States donated generously to the Central Park Conservancy. Indeed, they were so generous in their support that, by 2007, the New York City–based organization had raised more than $450 million for the park's restoration and maintenance. During the early twenty-first century, the conservancy—which since 1998 has officially managed the park for the city of New York—has provided an impressive 85 percent of Central Park's approximately $25 million yearly operating budget.

The conservancy's president from 1980 until 1996 was its founder, Elizabeth Barlow Rogers, who also served during the same period as Central Park administrator, a new position

STRAWBERRY FIELDS

The vast majority of the construction in Central Park during the last three decades has focused on renovation and rehabilitation of existing landscapes and structures. During the early 1980s, however, one significant new addition was made to the park: a 2.5-acre landscaped area known as Strawberry Fields. Designed as a living memorial to singer, composer, and peace activist John Lennon, who was shot to death in front of the nearby Dakota apartment building on December 8, 1980, the project was funded by Lennon's widow, artist and performer Yoko Ono.

Strawberry Fields, named for one of Lennon's most famous songs with the British rock group the Beatles, is a tear-shaped knoll (a small, rounded hill) located close to the park's West 72nd Street entrance. Together, Ono and landscape architect Bruce Kelly transformed the scruffy and long-neglected tract of land into the graceful Garden of Peace. The garden features flowers, trees, and shrubs donated by 150 different countries as well as hundreds of strawberry plants, and it has become one of Central Park's most popular and well-known attractions. The focal point of Strawberry Fields is a circular black-and-white mosaic fashioned by Italian craftsmen and presented to the park by the city of Naples. Inscribed in the mosaic is a single word, "Imagine," the title of Lennon's famous ode to world peace and understanding. Yoko Ono dedicated the mosaic and garden in a special ceremony held on October 9, 1985, which would have been Lennon's forty-fifth birthday. At the dedication, Ono quoted the famous Beatles song "Hey Jude," explaining that Strawberry Fields "is our way of taking a sad song and making it better."

created by New York City park commissioner Gordon Davis in 1979. Rogers, who holds degrees in art history and city planning, has a long-standing interest in Frederick Law Olmsted and is the author of several articles and books on the celebrated landscape architect. Yet despite Rogers's enormous respect for Olmsted and the Greensward Plan, notes Alan Tate in *Great City Parks*, as the head of the Central Park Conservancy she diplomatically "introduced an approach to rehabilitation that sought a balance between restoration of the Olmsted-Vaux design . . . on the one hand, but acknowledged contemporary demands on the other." Characterizing Central Park as first and foremost "a work of landscape art," in 1980 Rogers told a reporter that the conservancy's chief "purpose is to sustain the ingenious designs of Olmsted."

Nonetheless, she insisted that the conservancy had no intention of trying "to take the park back to the 19th century," explaining that "it has to be responsive to people's current needs." Accordingly, the conservancy has lovingly restored not only such original Olmsted-Vaux landscapes and structures as the Ramble, the Harlem Meer, the terrace, and the dairy but also popular attractions that were built after the designers' time, such as the Great Lawn, Heckscher Playground, and the park's 26 baseball diamonds.

During the three decades since the founding of the Central Park Conservancy, virtually every acre of the park has been affected in one way or another by the organization's efforts, which range from restoring elegant Bethesda Terrace (including a $7 million rehabilitation of the arcade's Minton tile ceiling) to reconstructing the bucolic pond and its surrounding landscape; from repairing aging benches, pathways, shelters, arches, and bridges to planting, pruning, and fertilizing the park's millions of flowers, trees, and shrubs. Today, Central Park draws an average of 25 million visitors each year who come to jog, bicycle, play sports, bird-watch, hear concerts,

Today Central Park attracts an average of 25 million visitors each year from all over the globe. More than 150 years after Olmsted and Vaux first created their visionary Greensward Plan, Central Park, with its breathtaking landscapes, graceful bridges, and other unique architectural structures, remains the most famous urban park in the United States and one of the most admired public spaces in the world.

or simply drink in Olmsted and Vaux's serenely beautiful and, thanks to the Central Park Conservancy, rejuvenated landscapes.

CHRONOLOGY

1844 William Cullen Bryant publishes a pro-park editorial in the *New York Evening Post.*

1851 Mayor Ambrose Kingsland urges the New York City Common Council to authorize the creation of a large public park in Manhattan.

1853 Seven hundred seventy-eight acres in midtown Manhattan are earmarked by the city for the "Central Park" project.

1856 The city of New York agrees to pay more than $5 million in compensation to owners of land on the Central Park site.

TIMELINE

1853
Seven hundred seventy-eight acres in midtown Manhattan are earmarked by the city for the "Central Park" project.

1856
The city of New York agrees to pay more than $5 million in compensation to owners of land on the Central Park site.

1853 — 1858

1857
Sixteen hundred residents are evicted from the Central Park site; workers begin clearing the site; the Board of Commissioners announces a public design competition for Central Park.

1858
Frederick Law Olmsted and Calvert Vaux win the design contest in April with their innovative Greensward Plan.

1857	Sixteen hundred residents are evicted from the Central Park site; workers begin clearing the site; the Board of Commissioners announces a public design competition for Central Park.
1858	Frederick Law Olmsted and Calvert Vaux win the design contest in April with their innovative Greensward Plan.
1858–1877	Central Park is constructed according to Olmsted and Vaux's Greensward Plan.
1859	Work on Bethesda Terrace begins.
1862	Bow Bridge is completed.
1863	Central Park's northern boundaries are extended northward from 106th Street to 110th Street, expanding the park to 843 acres.

1858 — **1980**

1863
Central Park's northern boundaries are extended northward from 106th Street to 110th Street, expanding the park to 843 acres.

1963
Central Park is declared a National Historic Landmark.

1858–1877
Central Park is constructed according to Olmsted and Vaux's Greensward Plan.

1980
Central Park Conservancy is founded.

1873	Emma Stebbins's *Angel of the Waters* sculpture is dedicated at Bethesda Terrace.
1877	Olmsted's long professional association with Central Park ends.
1926	Central Park's first equipped playground, Heckscher Playground, is constructed.
1934–1960	City parks commissioner Robert Moses oversees the construction of many athletic fields, playgrounds, and other building projects at Central Park.
1963	Central Park is declared a National Historic Landmark.
1960–1970s	Overuse and a fiscal crisis in New York City take their toll on Central Park.
1980	Central Park Conservancy is founded.
1981	Central Park Conservancy helps finance an extensive renovation of the park's deteriorating landscape and architecture.

GLOSSARY

abutment The part of a structure that supports the weight or pressure of an arch.

aesthetics The philosophical study of the qualities perceived in works of art.

arabesque A kind of ornate decoration often found in Islamic art in which leaves, branches, flowers, and geometric figures are intertwined in a complex pattern.

arboretum A tract of land on which trees and other woody plants are grown for display or study.

arcade A covered passageway.

architectural ornamentalism The addition of something to a building to enhance its appearance.

belvedere Literally, "beautiful view" in Italian; an architectural term for a structure designed to look out on a pleasing vista.

bucolic Pastoral.

cinquefoil An ornamental carving that consists of five intersecting arcs arranged in a circle.

comptroller A public official who maintains business accounts.

eminent domain The power of the state to seize private property for public use after compensation is provided to the owner.

encaustic tiles The patterns in this special type of ceramic tile are made by inlaying different colored clays into the body of the tile rather than by the usual method of applying a glaze on the surface.

folly In architecture, a whimsical structure meant to draw attention to an important view.

Gothic Revival architecture A popular style of architecture in North America and Europe during much of the nineteenth century, Gothic Revival imitated many of the elements of medieval European architecture, such as steeply pitched roofs, towers, and turrets.

grade To level or smooth to a desired or horizontal gradient or rate of inclination.

greensward Green, grassy turf.

hieroglyphics An ancient form of writing that uses pictures to represent words or sounds.

horticulture The art and science of cultivating flowers, vegetables, fruits, or ornamental plants.

knoll A small, rounded hill.

landscape architecture The planning and design of natural and built environments.

loggia A roofed porch with open sides.

mall A public walkway lined with shade trees; also called a promenade.

mosaic A decoration or picture composed of small pieces of inlaid stones, glass, or tile.

naturalistic Closely resembling nature.

obelisk A narrow, four-sided stone monument ending in pointed or pyramidal tops that was placed in pairs before the entrances to ancient Egyptian temples.

picturesque In landscape design, a type of landscape that has an air of mystery and wildness about it.

pocket park Also called vest-pocket parks, these very small open spaces are typically found in large cities.

schist The worn stubs of ancient mountain ranges; Manhattan Island's main bedrock, meaning the solid rock lying beneath the soil.

topography The physical features of an area.

verdant Covered with lush green grass or vegetation.

BIBLIOGRAPHY

Beveridge, Charles E., and Paul Rocheleau. *Frederick Law Olmsted: Designing the American Landscape.* New York: Universe, 1998.

Burns, Ric, and James Sanders. *New York: An Illustrated History.* New York: Alfred A. Knopf, 1999.

Burrows, Edwin G., and Mike Wallace. *Gotham: A History of New York City to 1898.* New York: Oxford University Press, 1999.

Fein, Albert, ed. *Landscape into Cityscape: Frederick Law Olmsted's Plans for a Greater New York City.* Ithaca, NY: Cornell University Press, 1967.

Gilfoyle, Timothy J. *Millennium Park: Creating a Chicago Landmark.* Chicago: University of Chicago Press, 2006.

Hall, Lee. *Olmsted's America: An "Unpractical" Man and His Vision of Civilization.* Boston: Little, Brown, 1995.

Kinkead, Eugene. *Central Park: 1857–1995. The Birth, Decline, and Renewal of a National Treasure.* New York: W.W. Norton, 1995.

Kowsky, Francis R. *Country, Park, & City: The Architecture and Life of Calvert Vaux.* New York: Oxford University Press, 1998.

Miller, Sara Cedar, *Central Park, an American Masterpiece: A Comprehensive History of the Nation's First Urban Park.* New York: Harry N. Abrams, 2003.

Rogers, Elizabeth Barlow. *Landscape Design: A Cultural and Architectural History.* New York: Henry N. Abrams, 2001.

Roper, Linda Wood. *FLO: A Biography of Frederick Law Olmsted.* Baltimore: The Johns Hopkins University Press, 1973.

Rosenzweig, Ray, and Elizabeth Blackmar. *The Park and the People.* Ithaca, NY: Cornell University Press, 1992.

Rybczynski, Witold. *A Clearing in the Distance: Frederick Law Olmsted and America in the Nineteenth Century.* New York: Scribner, 1999.

Simpson, Jeffrey. *Art of the Olmsted Landscape: His Works in New York City*. New York: New York City Landmarks Preservation Commission, 1981.

Spiegler, Jennifer C., and Paul M. Gaykowski. *The Bridges of Central Park*. Charleston, SC: Arcadia, 2006.

Stevenson, Elizabeth. *Park Maker: A Life of Frederick Law Olmsted*. New York: Macmillan, 1977.

Taylor, Dorceta E. "Central Park as a Model for Social Control: Urban Parks, Social Class and Leisure Behavior in Nineteenth-Century America." *Journal of Leisure Research* 31 (1999): 420–477.

FURTHER RESOURCES

Brawarsky, Sandee. *212 Views of Central Park: Experiencing New York City's Jewel from Every Angle.* New York: Stewart, Tabori & Chang, 2002.

Dunlap, Julie. *Parks for the People: A Story About Frederick Law Olmsted.* Minneapolis, MN: Carolrhoda Books, 1994.

Miller, Sara Cedar. *Central Park, an American Masterpiece: A Comprehensive History of the Nation's First Urban Park.* New York: Harry N. Abrams, 2003.

Mitchell, John G. "Frederick Law Olmsted's Passion for Parks." *National Geographic* (March 2005): 32–51.

WEB SITES

Central Park 2000
http://www.centralpark2000.com/index.html

Central Park Conservancy: The Official Website for Central Park
http://www.centralparknyc.org

Central Park History
http://www.centralpark.org/history

Elizabeth Barlow Rogers: The Central Park Story
http://www.elizabethbarlowrogers.com/lecture

Frederick Law Olmsted
http://www.fredericklawolmsted.com

Greensward Foundation: Bridges of Central Park
http://www.greenswardparks.org/books/bridges.html

National Association for Olmsted Parks
http://www.olmsted.org

New York Architecture: Olmsted and Vaux
http://www.nyc-architecture.com/ARCH/ARCH-OlmstedVaux.htm

PICTURE CREDITS

PAGE:

8 Mark Lennihan / AP Images
13 AP Images
18 Library of Congress, 2a14715r
22 Library of Congress, 3b09911
29 The Granger Collection
32 © Infobase Publishing
40 NYC Dept. of Parks & Recreation / AP Images
43 AP Images
48 Sarah A. Bonner Photography
52 New York Public Library
56 Collection of the New York Historical Society, Pro20–46–74435
61 Collection of the New York Historical Society, Pro20–46-Pre1860, Squatters Shacks
69 Library of Congress, 3a04850
76 Getty Images
80 © Corbis
84 Sarah A. Bonner Photography
91 Estate of Fred Stein / Art Resource, NY
97 Sarah A. Bonner Photography
100 © Bettmann / Corbis
102 Jerry Mosey / AP Images
106 Wally Santana / AP Images

INDEX

ABOUT THE AUTHOR

LOUISE CHIPLEY SLAVICEK received her master's degree in history from the University of Connecticut. She is the author of numerous periodical articles on historical topics and more than 20 other books for young people, including *Women of the American Revolution*, *Israel*, and *The Great Wall of China*. She lives in Ohio with her husband, James, a research biologist, and their two children, Krista and Nathan.

GREAT NECK LIBRARY
3 1266 21046 0507